Final Destiny
The Tragedy of Jewish Persecution

Final Destiny
The Tragedy of Jewish Persecution
Dr. Robert Mawire

ISBN 978-0-9671185-1-2

The Holy Bible, The New King James Version. Pocket Companion Bible. Thomas Nelson Publishers, Nashville, 1991.

COVER PHOTO CREDITS:

Yad Vashem (Holocaust Remembrance), Janusz Korczak Memorial, Israel Ministry of Tourism, www.goisrael.com.

The title of this book is not a play on words but a wake up call. It's an age-old dilemma for humankind: what to do with the Jews? Love them or hate them? This question of what to do with the Jews is fast bringing the world to the brink of a catastrophe of Biblical proportions. We're facing an apocalyptic prophecy for an all out nuclear holocaust. In the Middle East, lines are being drawn in the sand. The current rumblings echo the shock waves beginning at the epicenter in Jerusalem. We're on an imminent and inevitable countdown to Armageddon. The events in the Middle East swirling around us signal that the momentum is building. The world is accelerating towards a major cataclysm.

This book is written from an inerrant Biblical and historical perspective, based on verifiable facts, and infallible prophecies. Its foundation is the irrevocable and unconditional covenant God made regarding the land of Israel and the blessings of the Jews as a Chosen People. The consequence of violating the territorial integrity of the Promised Land as seen in the United Nations Resolutions puts us on a collision course with the Holy One of Israel.

Join me and travel through time to the dimension where God chose the Jewish people. Peer into this vortex and witness how this single divine act created a dilemma for all of humankind. Every kingdom has tried again and again to solve this problem. Each kingdom's solution focuses on exterminating the Jews to no avail.

A book like this is synergistic in nature, because it involves so many trans-generational writers, whose work provided the facts that demand a verdict. The facts contained in this book are too numerous to mention. These facts/historical events follow earth travelers who were eye witnesses to this unfolding saga. These insights are not new as "there is nothing new under the sun." Ancient Hebrew prophets predicted them and historians wrote accounts for future generations.

Since the problem is so complex and so deep, so illusive and so persuasive, I took the liberty to reiterate a certain salient matter to connect the dots. I expand on tangled theological issues and attempt to weave a clear panoramic picture and revelation. This demands immediate attention and urgent responses as this is the *final* dilemma in our generation.

I would like to especially express my gratitude to Shirley Langdon who has worked on this manuscript for years. I put it on the back burner, and she kept encouraging me to finish the task. It is now finished thanks to Shirley.

I am thankful to many of my Israeli Knesset friends who have shared with me their Messianic hope in the midst of rising anti-Semitism. The hope lives on.

It is difficult to find words that truly express my gratitude to Denise Mpinga for her tireless hard work of countless hours, putting finishing touches and making this work ready for publication.

As always my three sons Jonathan, Caleb and Stephen have been a tremendous support and encouragement. They have shared fully in my calling and vision.

I appreciate Dean and Joanna Spurlock for our many times in traveling to Israel and our prayers for the peace of Jerusalem.

I want to thank Larry Hopkins for the numerous times we have met to discuss the signs of the times and the centrality of Israel to the end game.

I especially appreciate Pastor Ray Bentley and his sweet wife, Vicki, for the encouragement they have been to me in our weekly long distance telephone visits to discuss this global dilemma. Iron sharpens iron, the deep calls unto the deep and it's precept upon precept. Invaluable time.

I am indebted to many friends for their encouragement and inspiration.

Most importantly I acknowledge my beloved wife Janet for typing countless drafts prayerfully and patiently without which this book could not be a reality.

To the living Jews, we apologize. We are inspired by your amazing saga, a story that must be told. A story, so extraordinary, so impossible, it defies simple explanation. It's only by the sovereignty of God you are here and we thank Him.

Finally, you my reader, of this revelation that demands an immediate attention and urgent response, it is my prayer that you will pray for the peace of Jerusalem as commanded in the Scriptures.

TABLE OF CONTENTS

THE GLOBAL DILEMMA – THE JEWISH PROBLEM

W e are now standing at the threshold of the most ominous event on the world stage, the battle of Armageddon. It's a drama that began four thousand years ago with the call of Abraham, the father of the Jewish people.

Humankind has been perplexed by the Jewish claim to divine election. What does it mean to be a Chosen People? Are the Jews above all other peoples and nations? Is this a bigoted falsification, a perpetuated snarl of passion for greatness, a historical paradox or a demonic delusion? Since its emergence in 4000 BC, historians have unsuccessfully tried to figure out this puzzle.

The oddities of Jewish culture and traditions have fascinated and upset Gentiles for centuries. Essentially, Gentiles are non-Jews. Jews are the children of Abraham through Isaac and Jacob. Jews have resisted Gentile influence throughout the ages. Their claim is they alone were chosen to live a unique, separated and exalted life under God. It's been a constant agitation on the world stage, culminating in collisions with pagan powers and ever increasing turbulence for such a small group of people.

THE HISTORICAL DIMENSION

The notion that one people among all peoples, tribes and languages claims a definitive and a futuristic Messianic domination was incomprehensible to the Ancient World. The Egyptians attempted to exterminate all the Jewish male babies and to oppress and destroy their future inheritance of the land of Canaan. The Assyrians destroyed the northern kingdom of Israel made up of the ten tribes and deported them to far away lands. They became the so called Lost Ten Tribes to this day.

The Babylonians destroyed the Temple and exiled Judah. The Persians took over from them and kept the Jews in subjugation. The Jews returned back to Jerusalem seventy years later to restore the

Temple on Mount Moriah. The Greeks came and attempted to Hellenize them. The Romans in AD 70 killed one million Jews defending the Temple and exiled the Jews into the Diaspora until 1948. In 1948, the modern state of Israel was born, inspired with the same ancient vision of a Messianic Kingdom that will rule the earth from Jerusalem. Since the rebirth of Israel, the Israelis have fought ten wars against 300 million Arabs who seek to wipe them off the face of the earth.

Let's take a quick tour through history's time capsule as summarized by Teaching Hearts.org:

The land known as Canaan encompassed Israel, the West Bank and Gaza, Jordan, and the southern portions of Syria and Lebanon.

Ancient Israel: Jerusalem, Capital of Israel.

- It was the site of the ancient Jewish temples which were destroyed twice. **Babylon** in 600 BC and by **Rome** in 70 AD.
- **The Temple Mount** or "the noble sanctuary" is made up of the following:
- **The Wailing Wall.** Ruins of the Jewish temple destroyed in 70 AD.
- **Dome of the Rock**. Islamic site built 687-691 AD.
- **Al-Aqsa Mosque**. Islamic temple at the Dome of the Rock

Ancient Egypt (2600–1500 BC): The Exodus.

Assyrian Empire (1170–612BC): The Ten Lost Tribes and "The Jews."

The Hittites invaded the north regions of Assyria and assimilated into the region.

- **The Ten Lost Tribes**. In 722 BC the Assyrian Empire, under King Shalmaneser V and Sargon II, captured the northern kingdom of Israel, destroyed the capital in Samaria.
- **The "Jews."** Only the tribes of Judah and Benjamin and their priests remained in the south and became "the Jews". They would be taken into exile by Babylon in 600 BC.

Babylonian Empire (609BC–539BC): Babylonian Exile.

- Babylon controlled Israel for seventy years (609–539 BC).
- **600 BC.** Daniel taken captive. Nabopolassar died and Nebuchadnezzar returned to Babylon by a short route across the desert.
- **597 BC.** More captives. Ezekiel and Jehoiachin
- **588–586 BC.** Siege of Jerusalem. Solomon's Temple in Jerusalem destroyed. Zedekiah and other captives taken.[6]

Medo-Persian Empire (539BC–331BC).

The Medo-Persian empire ruled from 539 BC to 331 BC. It defeated three nations:

- **Lydia.** 547 BC.
- **Babylon.** 539 BC.
- **Egypt.** 538 BC.

The leader was Cyrus the Great. He allowed the Jewish captives to go home with their sacred objects.

The Greek Empire (331BC–168BC).

It ruled from 331 BC to 168 BC. Under the leadership of Alexander the Great, the Greeks defeated Darius III of Persia.

The Roman Empire (168BC–476AD).

The Roman empire ruled from 168 BC to 476 A.D.

THE CHURCH DIMENSION

The presence of Jews in the Diaspora, in the Western World has created a vulgar xenophobia, subjecting them to animosity, prejudice and horrific suffering. Historically in the universe framed by Christian theology, anti-Semitism is eminently rooted in the accusation that the Jews were Christ-killers, enemies of God, and enemies of the human race considered utterly, inerrantly and inherently evil.

Christendom still perpetuates this anti-Semitic spirit ebbed in its psyche that Jews are God killers, sly, deceitful, pushy, arrogant, sycophantic, stingy, enemies of the Gospel, constantly undermining the Church. Its literature is vast on the subject, details endless. As we will discuss regarding the universality of this problem, a theology has developed to justify this perspective. In modern times, the Holocaust in which six million Jews were killed was just an eye opener to what Christendom is capable of doing to the Jewish people.

In essence, the Church's stance has been there is no atonement for the Jewish sin of killing Jesus of Nazareth, the Meshiach ben David, the Christ, the Son of God. The majority of the Church, if not the whole Church believes in Replacement Theology.

What is Replacement Theology? It's simple. The Jews have been replaced by the Church. There is no longer a Chosen People. The Church is the new Israel and the old Israel, the Jewish Israel is no longer relevant and acceptable to God. God hates the Jews. The Jews are cursed and must be killed. They are the rejected ones.

Replacement theology has created a god of its own liking: anti-Jewish, a god of crusades, inquisitions, pogroms and holocaust. Replacement theology falsely justifies the hatred of the Jews, as God Killers. The Church that hates Israel cannot belong to the Holy One of Israel, but becomes an instrument of Satan who truly hates Israel.

Theological Land Mines

The theological distance between the Church's interpretation and the Jewish interpretation of the same Scriptures can be bridged only by revelation.

The Church has developed three theological schools of thought, after the Reformation, regarding the Messianic kingdom and the Jews.

- The *spiritual replacement theology* teaches that the Messianic kingdom is God's current rule over those who submit to Him - the Elect.

- The *ecclesiastical school of thought*, another *replacement theology*, argues that the Church is the manifested Kingdom community. The Jews have been rejected as a people of God.

- The *eschatological school of thought* focuses on a future, end-of-time, literal Messianic Kingdom that will fulfill Jewish Messianic expectations. It is during the thousand-year reign of Christ on Earth when God resumes dealing with Israel.

Each school of thought has elements of truth, but not the whole truth. Half-truth is error. The spiritual replacement theology touches on what Jesus said in John 3:3: *"Unless one is born again, he cannot see the kingdom of God."* The ecclesiastical school is confirmed by Peter's statement in 1 Peter 2:9: *"But you are a chosen generation, a royal priesthood, a holy nation."* The eschatological school points to the future advent of the kingdom of God. This is the final manifestation of the Kingdom. The angels declared to the disciples at the ascension of Jesus in Acts 1:11: *"This same Jesus, who was taken up from you into heaven, will so come in like manner, as you saw Him go into heaven."*

The truth is a combination of all three schools of thought–which is that Jew and Gentile are now "one new man," brought together by Christ. Many in the Church also believe that in the future as the Church is raptured and meets the Lord in the air, that the anti-Christ will beat the hell out of the Jews before they are restored. The Church will be vindicated as the Jews receive their just reward–a hellish punishment waiting for them at the end of days.

THE TEMPLE DIMENSION

> *Now He said to me, 'It is your son Solomon who shall build My house and My courts; for I have chosen him to be My son, and I will be his Father. Moreover I will establish his kingdom forever, if he is steadfast to observe My commandments and My judgments, as it is this day."*
> 1 Chronicles 28:6-7.

In 1026 BC on Rosh Hashanah, King Solomon dedicated the completed Temple that his father King David prepared. Why Rosh Hashanah? Rosh Hashanah begins the Jewish New Year, and it is the day that the Jews believe that God began the creation of our universe. In religious and cultural terms, the Temple was to be a place where people could focus and meet with God. If you sinned, you would bring your sacrifices. It was the only place you could go to do this and where God's presence was manifested in a peculiar way. Most of the rituals centered on people receiving forgiveness.

The Temple is Judaism's central institution, and it constitutes the fundamental reason why God chose them from among the nations. Their objective was to build God an earthly house on Mount Moriah in Jerusalem, where He would put His name forever. The building of the Temple is a divine mandate to Israel. It is not a Zionist agenda.

The Gentile nations wanted to destroy the monopoly that Israel had with God who had dwelled with them from the beginning. The house of God was a confirmation of Israel's election. God chose them, and then He chose to live with them. Nobody else had a visible manifestation of the glory of the Creator God on the Earth.

When Israel compromised her covenant with God, then the conquests from the Gentile imperial powers began. Nebuchadnezzar destroyed Solomon's Temple, the First Temple. The Second Temple was built by Zerubbabel and expanded by King Herod and destroyed by Titus in AD 70.

The historical, political and religious issues regarding the Temple or Temple Mount as it's now known create insurmountable obstacles. Temple Mount is inciting Islamic fatalism and the worldwide call to jihad, which will culminate in the battle of Armageddon. Mr. Benny Elon, an Israeli politician is quoted as saying, "the Temple Mount is at the heart and is the most important issue in the conflict even though the majority of Jews as well as others do not understand it."

The Temple creates a controversy between Christians and Jews as Christendom wonders why Jews would build a temple on Mount Moriah after 2000 years without one. The Church is now the new replacement of the ancient Temple of God on Earth.

> *"Or do you not know that your body is the temple of the Holy Spirit who is in you, whom you have from God, and you are not your own."* 1 Corinthians 6:19.

The Church does not understand there are two temples, one is the spiritual house of Christ and the other is the physical house to be built on Mount Moriah.

The Temple creates even more of a dilemma as ancient predictions of a Third Temple start becoming a reality. In a survey taken in 2003, 53 percent of Israelis were in favor of building the Temple as a national symbol, uniting all the Jews worldwide. The desire to build the Temple is growing in momentum, and a prototype is already being built to prepare the priesthood for its coming. Mount Moriah will become ground zero in the conflict between Israel and the Islamic world.

In Ezekiel, Chapters 40 to 45, we see this ancient Hebrew prophet describing in marvelous detail, a glorious and extravagant Temple, built during Israel's rebirth. Most Biblical commentaries on

Ezekiel assume that the Temple he is describing is that of the Messiah. So for Christendom, there can't be another Temple before Jesus returns.

But if you look carefully at those passages, there is every indication that Ezekiel was describing a Temple that exists before Christ's return.

> *"He measured it on the four sides; it had a wall all around, five hundred cubits long and five hundred wide, to separate the holy areas from the common."* Ezekiel 42:20.

In Jesus' Kingdom, there won't be anything profane or unholy or common. The Messiah's Temple will be the Fourth Temple that comes from Heaven. And the book of Revelations confirms it clearly that a Third Temple will exist that does not include the court of the Gentiles, since that is where the Dome of the Rock now stands.

> *"Then I was given a reed like a measuring rod. And the angel stood, saying, "Rise and measure the temple of God, the altar, and those who worship there. But leave out the court which is outside the temple, and do not measure it, for it has been given to the Gentiles. And they will tread the holy city underfoot for forty-two months."* **Revelation 11:1–2.**

During the Millennium of Jesus' rule on Earth, there will be no court of the Gentiles. So what we understand from the Scriptures is that the Third Temple will be holy unto God and a reality before the coming of the Messiah and the Fourth Temple. The Third Temple will exasperate the age-old hatred of the Jews. It will be a great dilemma for evangelicals who are seeking reconciliation. Christendom will be offended with Jews returning to ancient Temple rituals and practices. The world will not understand why the Jews all over the globe practice such a primitive religion with its horrible blood sacrifices. Islam will be offended by Jews back on Mount Moriah. They will be isolated, hated and hunted for extermination as a pariah race of people. This single event will create a religious, political, social, economic crisis that will impact the whole world. It will be a universal crisis.

THE PROPHETIC DIMENSION TO THE DILEMMA

The Old Testament Hebrew scriptures contain 23,210 verses and 28 percent of these verses contain predictions. The New Testament has 7714 verses and 21.5 percent contain prophecies of the future. One third of the whole Bible contains predictions of the future of Israel, the Church and the world. Amazingly, that predicted future is upon us. It is firmly rooted in the controversial election of Israel as a Chosen People. The Incarnate Son of God who became the Son of David, the Messiah of Israel and the Savior of the world–Jesus, the coming King of Kings will rule the world from Jerusalem after judging the nations for how they treated Israel as prophesied.

> *"For behold in those days and at that time, when I bring back the captives of Judah and Jerusalem, I will also gather all nations, and bring them down to the valley of Jehosophat; And I will enter into judgment with them there on account of My people, My heritage Israel whom they scattered among the nations. They have also divided up My land."* Joel 3: 1-2.

The dividing of the Holy Land in the current 'Land for Peace' negotiations is the crux of the peace process. Land for Peace partitions God's land against the will of God who gave it to Abraham and his seed in an eternal covenant:

> *"The Lord said to Abraham…for all the land which you see I give to you and your descendants forever."* Genesis 13:15.

The Scriptures are clear that God will judge the nations for scattering His people. The violation of the territorial integrity of the Promised Land is a grave sin against God who defined the land's boundaries. The Lord will defend the land He gave to Abraham and his descendants, when He intervenes at the battle of Armageddon to rescue the Jewish people from extermination. The prophecies predict that the Antichrist will sit in the Third Temple claiming to be God. The Church will remain indifferent, since they believe they are the Temple of God, and God has nothing to do with the revival of the Jewish Temple and its rituals. Though the Apostle Paul clearly calls it the Temple of God in the New Testament:

> *"Who opposes and exalts himself above all that is called God or that is worshipped, so that he sits as God in the temple of God, showing himself that he is God….And then the lawless one will be revealed, whom the Lord will consume with the breath of His mouth and destroy with the brightness of His coming."* 2 Thessalonians 2: 4,8.

The leader of the New World Order will command the sacrifices to stop, as foretold by the prophet Daniel.

"He shall bring an end to sacrifices and offering." Daniel 9:27.

The Antichrist will desecrate the Temple on Mount Moriah as also foretold by the prophet Daniel:

"He even exalted himself as high as the Prince of the host and by him the daily sacrifices were taken away." Daniel 8:11.

It is imperative that we take a fresh look at what the Scriptures teach about Israel's past, present and future in the light of Biblical prophecy. Because this generation has an appointment with destiny and time is running out. The folly of most Christians is to ignore the Bible's inerrant and infallible words regarding Israel's place in the divine economy. Most Christians choose palatable words from the prophets for profit. The issue of Israel defines the endgame as Israel prepares to build the Third Temple in our day. The last players are moving into alignment on the world stage.

THE RISE OF THE GENTILE CHURCH AND THE END OF APOSTOLIC CHRISTIANITY

"For I know this, that after my departure savage wolves will come in among you, not sparing the flock. Also from among yourselves, men will rise up, speaking perverse things, to draw away the disciples after themselves .... Therefore watch and remember ... that for three years I did not cease to warn everyone night and day with tears." Acts 20:29.

The dialectical tension between Judaism and Christianity is based upon the faulty exegesis of the Gentile Church. With the death of the Apostles, the Gentile Church did not understand that God was going to hold back massive Jewish salvation until the fullness of the Gentiles was complete. The conflict started with what I like to call "the Judaizers and the Gentilizers." The former wanted to make Jews out of the Gentile Church. The pagan "Gentilizers" wanted to change the Jews to Gentiles.

The fact of the matter is the early Jewish Church brought the good news of Jesus Christ to the Gentile World. Gentiles were considered fellow citizens in the Commonwealth of Israel.

The Apostles taught from the Jewish Torah and sealed this testimony with their own blood. They made every effort not to burden the Gentile Church with the norms and regulations of traditional Judaism as taught by the Pharisees. Both Jews and Gentiles–born again, were a new creation. Jesus had removed the wall of partition between Jew and Gentile. Christian hostility toward the Jews is not part of the New Testament message, but a heresy born out of anti-Semitism.

The Apostle Paul was aware of the following facts:

"Blindness in part has happened to Israel, until the fullness of the Gentiles has come in." **Romans 11:25**.

"As concerning the gospel, they are enemies for your sake, but concerning the election they are beloved for the sake of the fathers." Romans 11:28.

"Do not boast against the branches [Jews]. But if you do boast, remember that you do not support the root, but the root supports you." Romans 11:18.

The Jewish people have partial blindness to the reality of Jesus as the Messiah because of God. Though the Torah confirms the suffering servant of God fulfilled in the person of Jesus Christ, their tradition denies it. As a result of two thousand years of hostility leveled at them by the Church, the Jewish collective conscience is now fulfilling Paul's prophecy: "as concerning the gospel they are enemies for your sakes."

It was two hundred to three hundred years later that the Church Fathers began to paganize the Church and to condemn the Jews. Justin Martyr in the Second century AD. and Origeon in the Third century accused Jews of plotting to kill Christians. Justin Martyr justified Christian anti-Semitism by urging that "Jewish cities be burned with fire and Jews be forbidden to go up to Jerusalem ... "for you have slain the just one and His prophets before Him, and now you reject those who hope in Him."

In 313 AD. through the Edict of Milan, Christianity became the state religion of the Roman Empire. The Church regarded this empowerment as the manifestation of the Kingdom of God on earth. The Church thought it was the New Israel, and the Jewish people were rejected as Christ-killers. The Church Fathers promoted anti-Semitism.

- Jerome (A.D. 347–419) said; "Jews are incapable of understanding the Scriptures."

- Hilary of Poitier in 367 called the Jews, "a perverse people forever accused by God."

- John Chrysostom (347–407) said "there could never be expiation for Jews and that God always hated them. It was incumbent on all Christians to hate Jews who were the assassins of Christ and worshipers of the devil."

Another example of this change in outlook was the Marcion Heresy, which advocated removing the Old Testament from the Holy Scriptures as irrelevant for the Church. Though Marcion was excommunicated, the truth is the Church adopted this attitude toward the Old Testament People of God.

And ironically, it was Jewish Rabbis who assisted the early translators of Scripture. The Church owes a great debt to these rabbis who suffered on our behalf to give us the word of God in our own languages. At every critical point, God has used the Jews to further His plans and purpose, beginning with Jesus of Nazareth.

JESUS' DIVINE MISSION TO THE JEWS

The prophet Zacharias, the father of John the Baptist, sets forth in matchless clarity God's plan for Israel, purposed in Jesus' first coming:

> *"Blessed is the Lord God of Israel, for He has visited and redeemed His people, And has raised up a horn of salvation for us in the house of His servant David, As He spoke by the mouth of His holy prophets, Who have been since the world began, that we should be saved from our enemies and from the hand of all who hate us, To perform the mercy promised to our fathers and to remember His holy covenant, the oath which He swore to our father Abraham: To grant us that we being delivered from the hand of our enemies, might serve Him without fear, in holiness and righteousness before Him all the days of our life."* Luke 1: 68-75.

Jesus' first coming was not a prelude to Israel's rejection, nor a postponement of His redemptive plan for Israel or her replacement by the Gentile Church. He came to show mercy to Israel and to fulfill His covenant promise to Abraham. God is not the author of confusion. Everything is on schedule, as He planned it before the foundation of the world.

Zacharias prophesied that the **dispensation of grace** would be the age when Israel would be restored to her God. Zacharias did not foresee the imminent transfer of Abraham's blessings from Israel to the Church. He saw Jesus' first advent as raising up "a horn of salvation for Israel in the house of His servant David."

However, the *replacement theology* argues that Israel rejected her Messiah, thus forfeiting her privileged position. They accuse Israel of being God-killers, as if it were the plan of the Jews. It was not so. Jesus died according to the Scriptures, as Peter told an audience of "thousands of Jews" on the day of Pentecost:

> *"Men of Israel, hear these words: Jesus of Nazareth, a Man attested by God to you by miracles, wonders, and signs*

which God did through Him in your midst, as you yourselves also know—Him, being delivered by the determined purpose and foreknowledge of God, you have taken by lawless hands, have crucified, and put to death: whom God raised up, having loosed the pains of death, because it was not possible that He should be held by it. For David says concerning Him:

> *'I foresaw the LORD always before my face,*
> *For He is at my right hand, that I may not be shaken.*
> *Therefore my heart rejoiced, and my tongue was glad;*
> *Moreover my flesh also will rest in hope.*
> *For You will not leave my soul in Hades,*
> *Nor will You allow Your Holy One to see corruption.*
> *You have made known to me the ways of life;*
> *You will make me full of joy in Your presence.'*

"Men and brethren, let me speak freely to you of the patriarch David, that he is both dead and buried, and his tomb is with us to this day. Therefore, being a prophet, and knowing that God had sworn with an oath to him that of the fruit of his body, according to the flesh, He would raise up the Christ to sit on his throne, he, foreseeing this, spoke concerning the resurrection of the Christ, that His soul was not left in Hades, nor did His flesh see corruption. This Jesus God has raised up, of which we are all witnesses. Therefore being exalted to the right hand of God, and having received from the Father the promise of the Holy Spirit, He poured out this which you now see and hear.

For David did not ascend into the heavens, but he says himself:

> *'The LORD said to my Lord,*
> *"Sit at My right hand,*
> *Till I make Your enemies Your footstool".*

"Therefore let all the house of Israel know assuredly that God has made this Jesus, whom you crucified, both Lord and Christ." Acts 2: 22-36.

Three thousand Jews believed in Jesus and were saved on the day of Pentecost, beginning our age of grace.

THE DESTRUCTION OF THE TEMPLE: THE PRELUDE TO JEWISH REJECTION

When the Temple was razed in 70 AD, it was the watershed event that humiliated Judaism. However, it was the validation of the Gospel: Jesus had predicted the destruction of the Temple and Jerusalem.

> *"Then as He went out of the temple, one of His disciples said to Him, "Teacher, see what manner of stones and what buildings are here!" And Jesus answered and said to him, "Do you see these great buildings? Not one stone shall be left upon another, that shall not be thrown down."* Mark 13:1-2.

The temple had been Judaism's symbol of spiritual arrogance, indeed a testimony of being God's Chosen People. With its splendor and beauty gone, the Jewish people were confused and degraded. The Gentile Church had a unique opportunity to return the debt of gratitude to the Jewish people, yet they chose to reject them. The *Bible people* had come to live among them to receive Christian hospitality. However, rather than welcoming them in the love of Christ, the Church greeted them with hostility.

In the consciousness of the Gentile body of Christ, the common-sense conclusion was that God had replaced the Chosen People with the elect among the nations. The displacement of Israel from the Holy Land evidenced to them God's hatred and rejection of Israel. This was a rationalistic conclusion.

The Gentile Church could not see God's wisdom and His example of divine election. The Diaspora experience of hostility preserved Israel in the wilderness of nations. That which the devil meant for evil, God used for His glory. God protected His Chosen People, from the natural processes of assimilation and absorption into the host countries.

The Gentiles' hostility had nothing to do with God's rejection of Israel. God foresaw it coming and factored it into His economics of redemption and salvation. Anti-Semitism was a perversion that grew out of the politics of Jewish absorption into the Church in the Greco-

Roman World, in the same places, where Paul had founded dynamic Churches.

The religious-political anti-Semitism intensified after state recognition of the Church by Rome. This is when the Church went into Babylonian exile—when it became the official religion of Rome. The Church lost its divine identity and its' Jewish roots. The lost Church in the lost world began to persecute the lost and wandering people of God in the Diaspora. Judaism and Christianity were on a collision course for the next two thousand years. The triumph of Christianity in the Roman World, the defeat and the subjugation of the Jewish people by Rome seemed to point to God's rejection. But God's ways are higher than our ways.

THE REAL MURDERERS OF JESUS

This confusion over who killed Jesus justified the Gentile Church's hostility towards the Jews, though the Scriptures are clear. The Jews did not kill Jesus. He was killed by our sins. He died that we may live.

The prophet Isaiah foretold the purpose of His death:

"Surely He has borne our griefs and carried our sorrows; Yet we esteemed Him stricken, smitten by God, and afflicted. But He was wounded for our transgressions, He was bruised for our iniquities; The chastisement for our peace was upon Him, and by His stripes we are healed. All we like sheep have gone astray; We have turned, everyone to his own way; And the LORD has laid on Him the iniquity of us all.

He was oppressed and He was afflicted, yet He opened not His mouth; He was led as a lamb to the slaughter, and as a sheep before its shearers is silent, So He opened not His mout.h" **Isaiah 53:4–7.**

Universal salvation for the Jews and Gentiles is in accepting Christ Jesus. All have sinned, both Jew and Gentile, and come short of the glory of God. The Gentilized Church behaves as if they did not fall short of the glory of God–that salvation was a reward for being better than Jews.

The lack of appreciation for our Jewish roots is inevitably caused by self-righteousness. During the Crusades, the Church encouraged pogroms and destruction of synagogues in Jerusalem and deportation of Jews from the West.

- St. Thomas Aquinas (1225–1274) demanded Jews be put to perpetual servitude. Every degrading law was passed against them as an accursed people.

- Pope Innocent said, "The Jews, against whom the blood of Jesus Christ calls out, although they ought not be killed, lest the Christian people forget the divine law. As wanderers, ought they to remain upon the Earth, until their countenance be filled with shame."

In every European country the Jews were consigned a life of shame and degradation, without security and protection, as the scum of the Earth. Martin Luther's solution to the Jews' dilemma was the opposite of his doctrine of grace and faith alone. He declared in his last sermon:

"First, their synagogues should be set on fire. Secondly, their homes should likewise be broken down and destroyed. Thirdly, they should be deprived of their prayer books, Talmud. Fourthly, their rabbis must be forbidden under threat of death to teach any more. Fifthly, passport and travel privileges should be absolutely forbidden to the Jews. Sixthly, they ought to be stopped from usury. Seventhly, let the young and strong Jews and Jewesses be given the flail, the ax, the hoe, the spade, the distaff, and spindle and let them earn the bread by sweat of their noses. We ought to drive the rascally lazy bones out of our system. Therefore, away with them. To sum up, dear princes and nobles who have Jews in your domains, **if this advice of mine does may all be free of this insufferable devilish burden–the Jews."**

On July 12, 1555, Pope Paul IV made a decree to restrict the Jews of the Holy Roman Empire to ghettos. England's defeat in 1588 of Phillip II and his Spanish Armada of Philip II ended the Inquisition. God opened up the New World for the persecuted people of God. Though formal and official anti-Semitism has ended, there is still much anti-Jewish sentiment in the Church.

God's Chosen People were divinely set apart to be a peculiar demonstration of the faithfulness of God–to encourage the Gentile Church. Surprisingly, it is precisely at this point that the Gentile Church parted ways with New Testament Christianity.

God chose the Jewish people to transmit His word to humankind. Jesus quoted the Old Testament. He authenticated the Torah. He read the Torah. He taught from the Torah.

The true Church of God is not anti-Jewish, because the real Church is a people brought into the Commonwealth of Israel. This is New Testament truth. Gentiles are adopted members of the family, and they share everything with the Jewish people:

- The Torah
- The God of Abraham, Isaac and Jacob
- The faith of Abraham and of the heroes of faith
- The irrevocable Old Testament covenants
- The same inspired Scriptures
- The Holy calling of the Creator God as a people
- The New Covenant through the blood of Jesus
- Eternal election of God
- Salvation through Jesus by grace alone
- The hope of the Messianic Kingdom
- The hope of the Resurrection of the Dead

These fundamental elements bind the Christians and Jews together. The eschatological hope of the Old Testament is the coming of the Messiah.

As Christians, the New Testament is a historical record that Jesus fulfilled prophecy on Calvary's cross. He is the Savior of the world. The New Testament is a perfect continuance of the Torah as a literal fulfillment of all Scriptures, through the person of Jesus Christ.

THE SUFFERING SERVANT

T he hostile and ambivalent relationship between Christianity and Judaism centers on different interpretations of the same Holy Scriptures. The prime focus of the Old Testament is the coming of the Messiah. The Jews reject the incarnation and the deification of Jesus of Nazareth, even though contemporary eyewitnesses documented that He fulfilled all the Messianic prophecies. The Apostle Peter called His fellow Jews to accept their long-awaited Messiah, Jesus of Nazareth.

> *"Men of Israel, hear these words: Jesus of Nazareth, a Man attested by God to you by miracles, wonders, and signs which God did through Him in your midst, as you yourselves also know–Him, being delivered by the determined purpose and foreknowledge of God, you have taken by lawless hands, have crucified, and put to death; whom God raised up, having loosed the pains of death, because it was not possible that He should be held by it."* Acts 2:22–24.

The early Apostles saw the fulfillment of Isaiah 53 in the death and resurrection of Jesus:

> *"Who has believed our report? And to whom has the arm of the LORD been revealed? For He shall grow up before Him as a tender plant, and as a root out of dry ground, He has no form or comeliness; And when we see Him, There is no beauty that we should desire Him. He is despised and rejected by men, a Man of sorrows and acquainted with grief, and we hid, as it were, our faces from Him; He was despised, and we did not esteem Him.*

> *Surely He has borne our griefs and carried our sorrows; Yet we esteemed Him stricken, Smitten by God, and afflicted. But*

He was wounded for our transgressions,, He was bruised for our iniquities; The chastisement for our peace was upon Him, And by His stripes we are healed. All we like sheep have gone astray; We have turned, every one, to his own way; And the LORD has laid on Him the iniquity of us all.

He was oppressed and He was afflicted, Yet He opened not His mouth; He was led as a lamb to the slaughter, And as a sheep before its shearers is silent, So He opened not HIs mouth, He was taken from prison and from judgment, and who will declare His generation? For He was cut off from the land of the living; For the transgressions of My people He was stricken. And they made His grave with the wicked – But with the rich at His death, Because He had done no violence, Nor was any deceit in His mouth.

Yet it pleased the LORD to bruise Him; He has put Him to grief. When You make His soul an offering for sin, He shall see His seed, He shall prolong His days, and the pleasure of the LORD shall prosper in His hand. He shall see the labor of His soul, and be satisfied. By His knowledge My righteous Servant shall justify many, For He shall bear their iniquities. Therefore I will divide Him a portion with the great, And He shall divide the spoil with the strong, Because He poured out His soul unto death, And He was numbered with the transgressors, And He bore the sin of many, And made intercession for the transgressors." **Isaiah 53: 1–12.**

In his prediction of the Messiah, Isaiah presents details that the Jewish interpretation has failed to explain. Instead, modern Jewish theologians identify *Israel* as the suffering servant of God. This passage is too particular in describing an individual personage, His birth and His death. Isaiah says, "He will bear the iniquities of many." Israel is not the savior of the World. *Jesus* is the savior who bore the sins of the World.

All the events predicted and elaborated by Isaiah the prophet concerning the coming Messiah, the servant of the Lord, were fulfilled. Isaiah's prediction clearly shows that Calvary is an event in eternity planned in the heart of God, which took place at the appointed time in history.

The prophetic perspective anticipated Israel's rejection of the Messiah, His death and His resurrection. In a few generations, the extravagant hodge podge and trivial accusations against Jesus and His disciples proliferated to encompass all future generations of Jews. The corporate rationale of Judaism is to preserve national unity in anticipation of a future Messianic fulfillment.

Jesus did not reject the Jews as a people. He rejected the Pharisaical Judaism as a perversion of the Torah. He rejected a false religiosity of forms and rituals. Instead, He called Israel back to her God. He died for the sin of Israel when they rejected Him. Their sin has been paid for in full. He commissioned His disciples to be His witnesses beginning with His Chosen People in Jerusalem.

Jesus said, *"But you shall receive power when the Holy Spirit has come upon you; and you shall be witnesses to Me in Jerusalem, and in all Judea and Samaria, and to the end of the earth."* Acts 1:8.

Jesus did not separate the Gospel from the history of Israel's covenant with God. He is the central figure of the Old Testament, and the fulfillment of the hope of Israel. He is Israel's kinsman redeemer. He is the High Priest in the order of Melchizedek, who opened a new and living way into the Holy of Holies. He is the Son of David and the Holy One of Israel. He is the Messiah of Israel. He was born as King of the Jews. He died as King of the Jews and He is coming back, as King of the Jews to Jerusalem.

JESUS: THE FULFILLMENT OF OLD TESTAMENT PROPHECIES

The First Coming of the Messiah established the spiritual Kingdom in the hearts of humankind. The citizens of His Kingdom must be born again from above.

"Jesus answered and said to him, 'Most assuredly, I say to you, unless one is born again, he cannot see the kingdom of God." John 3:3.

The Second Coming will usher the millennial phase of the Kingdom. All prophecies must have a spiritual and a material fulfillment in history. First, He came to remove iniquity from His people. This is the first phase in the redemption and restoration of all things.

The Second Coming will fulfill Jewish Kingdom expectations, the consummation of all things and the judgment of all humankind. The Jewish people do not see how the Kingdom Jesus proclaimed in the Gospel brings to reality the reign of the Messiah that the prophets predicted.

Both comings have been prophesied, one as the suffering servant and the other as the King of the Jews, heir to the throne of David.

Understanding Prophecy

The Hebrew word "Nabi" describes a holy man who received prophecies. Holy men, the Old Testament prophets, revealed the future from God and were passive instruments in the transmission of His revelation.

Prophecy is God's revelation in human language. The Nabis' personality was set aside to preserve the purity of the revelation from fallible human nature. You have to set aside your preconceived notions, being not only a believer but a student of the Word. The way to understand biblical prophecies is through prayer and study. The many published biblical commentaries give you pieces in a complex puzzle.

God hides His secrets, and wise men seek them. If you don't keep seeking, it won't be given to you. God doesn't want to hide anything. He just requires you to be an active participant in your faith walk, to be engaged and committed, seeking the truth.

> *"Look, I go forward, but He is not there. And backward, but I cannot perceive Him; When He works on the left hand, I cannot behold Him; When He turns to the right hand, I cannot see Him. But He knows the way that I take."* **Job 23: 8–10.**

> *"For there is nothing hidden which will not be revealed, nor has anything been kept secret, but that it should come to light. If anyone has ears to hear, let him hear."* **Mark 4:22–23.**

The Jews expected the Messiah to establish the Davidic Kingdom. They believed the Son of David, the Messiah, would appear to His people in the order of the predicted events as they understood it. He then would set up the Messianic Kingdom. Here's how Jesus fulfills Old Testament prophecies.

- He would be born of the seed of a woman. Genesis 3:15; Galatians 4:4.
- He would be born of the seed of Abraham. Genesis 12:1-3; Matthew 1:1.

- He would be born of the seed of Isaac. Genesis 17:19; Matthew 1:2.

- He would be descended from the tribe of Judah. Genesis 49:10; Luke 1:32–33.

- He would be heir to the throne of David. Isaiah 9:7; Luke 1:32–33.

- He would be born of a virgin. Isaiah 7:14; Luke 1:26-30.

- He would appear at the time designated for the Messiah's birth. Daniel 9:25; Luke 2:1–2.

- His birthplace would be in Bethlehem. Micah 5:2; Luke 2:4–7

- Innocent babies would be slaughtered. Jeremiah 31:15; Matthew 2:16–18).

- He would be called out of Egypt. Hosea 11:1; Matthew 2:14–15.

- A forerunner would precede Him. Isaiah 40:3-5; Luke 7:24–27.

- He would minister in Galilee. Isaiah 9:1–2; Matthew 4:13–17).

- He would come to heal the broken hearted. Isaiah 61:1–2; Luke 4:18–19.

- He would enter Jerusalem in triumph, riding on an ass's colt. Zechariah 9:9; Mark 11:7–11.

- His own people would reject Him. Isaiah 53:3; John 1:11.

- He would be a priest after the order of Melchizedek. Psalm 110:4; Hebrews 5:5–6.

- He would be a light to the Gentiles. Isaiah 42:6, 60:3; Luke 1:32–33).

- He would be the suffering Servant of the Lord. Isaiah 42:1, 19: 52:13; 53:11–12.

- He would be sold for thirty pieces of silver, which would be used to buy the potter's field. Zechariah 11:12–13; Matthew 26:27.

- He would be betrayed by a friend. Psalm 41:9; Luke 22:47–48.

- He would be accused by false witnesses. Psalm 35:11; Mark 14:57–58.

- He would remain silent under judgment Isaiah 53:7; Mark 15:4–5.

- He would be spat upon and flogged. Isaiah 50:6; Matthew 26:6–7.

- He would be mocked. Psalm 22:7–8; Luke 23:35.

- His flesh would be pierced. Psalm 22:16; Zechariah 12:10; John 19:34, 20:27.

- He would be crucified with transgressors. Isaiah 53:12; Mark 15:27–28.

- He would pray for His enemies. Psalm 109:4; Isaiah 53:12; Luke 23:24.

- He would be given vinegar and gall to drink. Psalm 69:21; Matthew 27:34.

- His garments would be parted among others and lots would be cast for His robe. Psalm 22:1; Matthew 27:35.

- His life would be a vicarious sacrifice for others. Isaiah 53:3; Romans 5:6–8.

- None of His bones would be broken. Psalm 34:20; John 19:32–36.

- He would be buried with the rich. Isaiah 53:9; Matthew 27:57–60.

- He would raise from the dead. Psalm 16:10, 49:15; Mark 16:6–7.

- He would ascend to the right hand of God as Savior. Psalm 68:18; Mark 16:19.

THE FULFILLMENT OF GOD'S PROMISES TO ABRAHAM

Jesus was a fulfillment of the promise God made to Abraham–through Him all the families of the Earth would be blessed. The destiny of the seed of Abraham is to bring blessings to the rest of humankind. God chose them to be channels of His blessings. The historical implications of Jesus' being a fulfillment of the Abrahamic covenant are universally realized in the inclusion of Gentiles. The Gentiles are now made joint heirs with Christ Jesus. Through rebirth they have been adopted into the family that is chosen to inherit the blessings of Abraham.

"For the promise that he would be the heir of the world was not to Abraham or to his seed through the law, but through the righteousness of faith. For if those who are of the law are heirs, faith is made void and the promise made of no effect, because the law brings about wrath; for where there is no law there is no transgression.

Therefore it is of faith that it might be according to grace, so that the promise might be sure to all the seed, not only to those who are of the law, but also to those who are of the faith of Abraham, who is the father of us all." **Romans 4: 1–16.**

The Apostle Paul makes it clear that the fulfillment of the promise is in accordance with grace. So that it may be certain to all the descendants, not only to those who are of the *law* (Jews) but also to those who are of the *faith* of Abraham, the father of us all. How can he be father of us all if the Jews are rejected? It is only by grace.

The Abrahamic covenant is the basis of both the Jewish and the Gentile relationship with God. The Law was the basis of fellowship in the context of the Mosaic covenant in the Old Testament. In the New Testament, Jesus is the mediator. We have fellowship with God through Him. God replaced the Law with grace.

"And of His fullness we have all received, and grace for grace, for the law was given through Moses, but grace and truth came through Jesus Christ." **John 1:16–17.**

The Jews received grace upon grace. Jesus fulfilled the Law for them. He made them acceptable in the beloved. He universalized the grace to include Gentiles. He removed the wall of partition between Jews and Gentiles and made both **"one new man."**

However, the Gentile Church built the wall right back up to isolate Jews. The Church has demonized the Jews and allegorized the prophecies concerning them. In effect, it makes the promises of the Old Testament just mystical experiences, anti-Semitizes Christianity and makes it Hellenized i.e. Greek, replacing Israel with the Church and promoting Jewish persecution.

The election of Israel is eternal. However, all Israel is not the Israel of God, only the elect among them—the faithful remnant.

Nevertheless, all *natural* Israel is blessed with all the natural blessings bestowed upon Abraham, Isaac and Jacob.

According to Paul's letter to the Romans, there is in every generation a remnant of the true Israel of God.

"God has not cast away His people whom He foreknew, or do you not know what the Scripture says of Elijah, how he pleads with God against Israel, saying, "LORD, they have killed Your prophets and torn down Your altars, and I alone am left, and they seek my life? But what does the divine response say to him? "I have reserved for Myself seven thousand men who have not bowed down the knee to Baal." Even so then, at this present time there is a remnant according to the election of grace." **Romans 11:2–5.**

The Jewishness of Jesus

Though the Church accepts Jesus as the Messiah, it minimizes His Jewishness. It is His Jewishness that is fundamental and essential and critical to His Messianic mission. He is the Son of David. He is the Messiah of Israel.

"But one of the elders said to me, 'Do not weep, Behold the Lion of the tribe of Judah, the Root of David, has prevailed to open the scroll. Revelation 5:5.

"And in that day there shall be a Root of Jesse, Who shall stand as a banner to the people; For the Gentiles shall seek Him, And His resting place shall be glorious." Isaiah 11:10.

The Hellenistic or Greek and Roman image of Jesus is not authentic. He was not a Westerner. He was a Hebrew, Messiah and Savior of the World. He lifted Jewishness to new heights of glory.

Jesus' ancestry gives Him His identity. His Jewish roots shaped His destiny. The only way to understand Jesus of Nazareth is to see Him in the context of His Jewishness. God became a Jew, the son of Abraham and dwelt among men.

Son of David – The Royal Lineage

The book of Matthew gives us Jesus' royal lineage. His ancestry gives Him divine right to the throne of David. He is King of the Jews. He adhered to Hebrew Scriptures, sang Hebrew songs, and celebrated

Hebrew feasts. The man Jesus we preach as Savior, raised from the dead and seated at the right hand of God, is still the Son of David, a King of the Jews. He is coming back to the ancient city of David. He will rule the world during the Millennium from Jerusalem. How can we love Jesus and not love His people?

The moment we try to divorce Jesus from His physical, material and homogeneous Jewish flesh and blood roots, we become apostate. The spirit of the Antichrist denies that Jesus came in the flesh. What flesh? Jewish flesh! Salvation comes from the Jews.

The disciples were eyewitnesses, together with all the Jews in Jerusalem. On the day of Pentecost, three thousand Jews believed in Jesus and were saved. The whole Apostolic Church in Jerusalem was Jewish. All the early missionaries to the Gentile world were Jewish. We received the Torah from the Jews. God inspired Jewish writers to write both the Old and New Testaments.

> *"If someone says, 'I love God,' and hates his brother, he is a liar; for he who does not love his brother whom he has seen, how can he love God whom he has not seen?"* 1 John 4:20.

The people of God need to have a clear understanding that we cannot hate the Jewish people and call ourselves children of Abraham by faith. The Jewishness of Jesus confirms God's choice of Abraham and His seed. Jesus commanded the Church after His resurrection to begin the Apostolic mission in Jerusalem. He prioritized the restoration of Israel to her God, during this age of grace. God did not just pick Abraham to use His seed to bring forth His plan in the person of Jesus. God is not a user. God is a lover. He loves Israel like a father loves His children.

> *"You are the children of the LORD your God; you shall not cut yourselves nor shave the front of your head for the dead. For you are a holy people to the LORD your God, and the LORD has chosen you to be a people for Himself, a special treasure above all the peoples who are on the face of the earth."* Deuteronomy 14:1–2.

Israel is called "children of the Lord your God," and "an holy people unto the Lord." Jesus came to impart holiness and eternal sonship to all those who believe in Him.

> *"But as many as received Him, to them He gave the right to become children of God, to those who believe in His name."* John 1:12.

Jesus is the second Adam, the Father of the new creation. Jesus is the fulfillment of the Old Testament Kingdom covenant with David. He is the long-awaited king of Israel. The land of Israel belongs to Him. He will return to defend Jerusalem at the last battle, the battle of Armageddon.

THE DEITY OF JESUS

The idea that the Holy God could exist in the person of Jesus is an offense to Jews. Jewish monotheism rejects the Christian doctrine of the Trinity as blasphemy. The word "trinity" is not in the Bible, although it is central to understanding the Godhead–The Father, The Son and the Holy Spirit.

As modern Judaism teaches, Christianity is a new form of religion unrelated to the Old Testament. Jews have problems with the incarnation and deification of Jesus of Nazareth. God could not appear as an ordinary man. He is abstract. Jesus was too human to be God incarnate. In addition, the hiatus between the ascension and the second coming of Jesus poses a stumbling block to the Jewish understanding of the Messianic mission and kingdom.

However, Christianity at its core is solidly built upon the historical fulfillment of Old Testament Messianic predictions. It is the fulfillment of the Torah.

> *"For unto us a Child is born, Unto us a Son is given; And the government will be upon His shoulder. And His name will be called Wonderful, Counselor; Mighty God, Everlasting Father, Prince of Peace."* Isaiah 9:6.

> *"Behold, the days are coming,"* says the LORD, *'That I will raise to David a Branch of righteousness; A King shall reign and prosper, And execute judgment and righteousness in the earth. In His days Judah will be saved, And Israel will dwell safely; Now this is His name by which He will be called: THE LORD OUR RIGHTEOUSNESS."* Jeremiah 23:5–6.

The Old Testament abounds with prophetic paradoxes or seeming contradictions about the Messiah, who would be both:

- Begotten of God, yet God
- Son of God, yet Son of man

- Chosen of God, yet forsaken
- Suffering Servant, yet Everlasting Father
- Son of David, yet David's Lord
- Seed of the woman, yet seed of Abraham
- Chief cornerstone, yet a stone of stumbling or offense
- Messiah of Israel, yet rejected of Israel
- High Priest, yet from the tribe of Judah
- Born in Bethlehem, but "called a Nazarene," and elsewhere "called out of Egypt"

It is impossible for any human being to fulfill these prophecies. Who could untangle these contradictory realities?

The Jews of Jesus' day asked Him, *"Tell us plainly if you are the Christ."* And what lies at the crux of this issue is that there is not a place in the Bible where Jesus says He's God. He never denied that He was God. He accepted worship as God. He forgave sins as God. He always refers to His Father and that's why a lot of Jews and Christians have a problem with worshipping Jesus as God.

In addition, another seeming conflict comes with the Shema, the unadulterated basis of monotheism:

"Here O' Israel, the Lord Your God is One."

This declaration that the Lord Your God is One adds to the real conundrum, how you can conceive the three in one? It's an extremely difficult concept except for the overwhelming Biblical evidence, which has from the beginning shown the plurality of the Godhead.

"In the beginning, Elohim created the heavens and the earth ...." Genesis 1:1. The word Elohim or God as we say it is actually plural in the Hebrew.

"Then Elohim said, 'Let Us make man in Our image, according to Our likeness." Genesis 1:26

The Apostle Paul explains in his letter to Timothy the mystery of the Trinity:

"And without controversy great is the mystery of godliness: God was manifested in the flesh, justified in the Spirit, seen by angels, preached among the Gentiles, believed on in the world, received up in glory." 1 Timothy 3:16.

It is a historical fact that through the incarnation, the second Person of the Godhead entered into a new dimension of human existence when the Word became flesh and dwelt among us.

"And the Word became flesh and dwelt among us, and we beheld His glory, the glory as of the only begotten of the Father, full of grace and truth." John 1:14.

Think about this. Jesus was actually born during the Feast of Tabernacles (August/September), not in December as so many of us celebrate. Jesus was the fulfillment of the Feast of Tabernacles, a divine appointment with humankind. God came down and tabernacled (dwelt) among us. The Feast of Tabernacles celebrates Israel's deliverance from slavery. Jesus' birth celebrates our spiritual deliverance. First the natural, then the spiritual.

This feast requires the Jews to leave their houses and go outside and live in booths for a week–they have to live outside of their normal environment. Jesus came from heaven, lived outside his natural environment and dwelt in a human body to save us.

"He was in the world, and the world was made through Him, and the world did not know Him. He came to His own, and His own did not receive Him." **John 1:10–11.**

During His earthly ministry Jesus effectively expressed the will of His Father, as the "only begotten Son." Scripture, in almost every case, when God refers to His only begotten Son, applies to Jesus' human existence. *"You are My Son, Today I have begotten You."* Psalm 2:7; Acts 13:33.

As the pre-existent Word, He was the Creator of the world and of all things visible and invisible. Jesus was not simply an extraordinary person. He is God. Gabriel told Mary clearly that Jesus was to be called *"the Son of the Highest ... the Son of God."* Luke 1:32–35.

The incarnation was a willing obedience to the Father. Jesus emptied himself of deity and humbled Himself by putting on the form of a man. Paul says,

"Let this mind be in you which was also in Christ Jesus, who, being in the form of God, did not consider it robbery to be equal with God, but made Himself of no reputation, taking the form of a bondservant, and coming in the likeness of men. And being found in appearance as a man, He humbled Himself, and became obedient to the point of

death, even the death of the cross. Therefore God also has highly exalted Him, and given Him the name which is above every name..." **Philippians 2:5–9.**

The incarnation was for the purpose of redemption of the seed of Adam. The Son of God became the Son of Man, so that the sons of men may become sons of God. The last Adam needed to take a body similar to ours in order to become our kinsman redeemer. He came to give us back our sonship identity and the image of God we lost through sin.

As God incarnate and the second Adam, Jesus was both fully human and fully divine. He had perfect human nature, and all that was characterized of unfallen man was found in Him. The eternal significance of Jesus' virgin birth was His holy nature, which was needed for redemption and atonement for sin. He was *"the Lamb of God, which taketh away the sin of the World."* John 1:29.

As Mary, His mother, said, *"Blessed is the Lord God of Israel, for He has visited and redeemed His people."* **Luke 1:68.**

Still this day Jews are asking, "Who is Jesus of Nazareth?"

This is the greatest question in all of history. Your eternity depends upon it. It is a simple question with profound consequences. Each person must answer this eternal question for himself or herself, whether Jew or Gentile. To know Him is life eternal. He came to restore to humankind, the God-image we lost through sin. An encounter with Jesus of Nazareth is a confrontation with God.

UNDERSTANDING THE ABRAHAMIC COVENANT

"Now the LORD had said to Abram: 'Get out of your country, from your family and from your father's house, to a land that I will show you, I will make you a great nation; I will bless you and make your name great; And you shall be a blessing. I will bless those who bless you, and I will curse him who curses you; and in you all the families of the earth shall be blessed. Genesis 12:1-3.

The call to separation is the essence of the Abrahamic covenant. The separation and holiness position of the people of God is the theme that binds all the covenants. Abraham and his seed were to be a holy people whose existence was to show forth the glory of God to all the families of the Earth, and to call a people unto God from every tongue and nation. Jesus came to impart His holiness, His power to live a holy life and His grace to overcome the world, in order to fulfill the divine destiny.

The essence of the new covenant at the present age of grace is described in Hebrews 8:16, *"This is the covenant that I will make with them after those days, says the Lord: I will put My laws into their hearts, and in their minds I will write them…"*

The believers are called out or separated like Abraham of old, for God has said to them; *"I will be their God, and they shall be My people."* 2 Corinthians 6:1:6.

In order to come to terms with the complex global problem—the Jewish issue—one has to go to the origin of this people. Origin determines destiny. God created the Jewish problem. He called Abraham and His seed to be separate from all humankind. He made a commitment to Abraham in an eternal and unilateral covenant, as an act of grace. Abraham found favor in the sight of God.

God initiated the *berith* with Abraham. The word *berith*, translated "covenant," appears in the Old Testament 278 times—97 times in the first five books—signifying the importance of this relationship. God's covenant with Abraham constitutes the basis of all His redemptive dealings with the world thus consummated in the new covenant.

The Abrahamic covenant is not based upon mutuality and reciprocity, because during the *karath berith* ceremony–the act of cutting covenant–Abraham went into a deep sleep. God made a one-sided covenant. He committed Himself to Abraham and His seed in an eternal relationship to be his shield and great reward. God has an indisputable prerogative to choose whom He will.

The Abrahamic covenant irreversibly affirms the absolute sovereignty of God. There is a remarkable harmony between the Abrahamic covenant and the Messianic covenant, because the latter is the fulfillment of the former.

What we have to grasp, then, is that our God-given responsibility is to show love to the Jewish people in spite of their rejection of Jesus. The Church is God's agent of carrying the Good News to the Jews. The New Testament presents all believers, Jew and Gentile, as heirs of the Abrahamic covenantal promises.

The Abrahamic covenant has three essential dimensions:

- The seed. Genesis 13:16; 15:5.
- The blessings. Genesis 12:3; 17:7.
- The land. Genesis 12:2; 13:15; 15:5–8; 17:6–8.

Natural and national Israel has a distinguished destiny that includes the land promised to Abraham. God promised the land to Israel as an everlasting heritage.

> *"Declaring the end from the beginning, and from ancient times things that are not yet done ... My counsel shall stand, and I will do My pleasure."* Isaiah 46: 10.

THE LAW AND TALMUDIC TRADITIONS

The Mosaic Law includes the set of Ten Commandments and Levitical regulations governing social and dietary lifestyle that Moses received from God on Mt. Sinai. Exodus 20: 1–17.

With the crumbling of the Jewish state in AD 70, Jews were scattered throughout the wilderness of nations for their sins. Traditional Judaism began to be scrutinized, analyzed, criticized, contested and either overthrown or adversely transformed into modern

Judaism. Judaism has no message without prophets, priests and sacrifices on Mount Moriah. Authentic Judaism is Biblical.

The destruction of the Temple, the removal of the priesthood and the shift in the locus of Jewish religion from centralized public services to the Diaspora resulted in gradual disillusion and despair among Jews. The Talmudic traditional dogmas created by the Jewish teachers were then established as a temporary order, out of the chaos and void in the Diaspora.

The problem with Judaism is an authority vacuum. Only prophets could speak with divine authority. No rabbi has divine authority. This creates an institutional crisis. Where is the God of Abraham? Where is The Holy One of Israel?

The Talmud emphasizes oral law, a method of interpreting the Scriptures to adapt to changing circumstances. This method conflicts with the unchangeableness of God's word. His word and its meaning are eternal.

Jesus says, *"Heaven and Earth will pass away, but My words will by no means pass away."* Matthew 24:35.

Today the Talmud is the supreme surrogate for the Torah. The Talmud is the recorded debates, observations and pious expositions of the academies in Babylon, Egypt and Palestine, finally set in writing. It is a comprehensive hedge of prohibitions, customs and traditions of people. It separated the Jews in the Diaspora from their Gentile neighbors. The real essence of Israel's divine election is her being in the world—not these visible traditions.

Jesus rejected the Judaism that was based upon "the traditions of men and doctrines of demons." He didn't reject the Jewish Torah, which He called, the Holy Scriptures. Jesus rejected their systematic theology and interpretation. Today Jesus rejects the traditions of the whore Church that rejects Israel as God's Chosen People.

Jesus came to fulfill the legal requirements of the Law, so that His people through His name might appropriate the blessings of Abraham. The Law requires the daily shedding of blood to cover the sins of the people. Blood sacrifices were a basis of Israel's relationship with God. He is the end of the Law and not the removal of the Law.

Jesus was the end of the Law, because now the Law is fulfilled in the life of the believer, through the in-dwelling Christ. The Law Giver now living in the hearts of His People. Jesus rejected the beggarly elements of Judaism as the way to God. Jesus is now the way to God for Israel and all humankind:

> *"Jesus said to him, 'I am the way, the truth, and the life. No one comes to the Father except through Me."* John 14:6.

> *"Do not think that I came to destroy the Law or the Prophets, I did not come to destroy but to fulfill."* Matthew 5:17.

Gentile Inclusion Under Abraham's Covenant

> *God is obligated by His covenant to Israel, forever. David said, "He remembers His covenant forever, the word which He commanded, for a thousand generations, The covenant which He made with Abraham, and His oath to Isaac, and confirmed it to Jacob for a statute, to Israel as an everlasting covenant."* **Psalm 105: 8–10.**

Moses described the Abrahamic covenant as *"the covenant and the mercy which He swore to your* fathers." Deuteronomy 7:12. Israel's unconditional election is an act of God's mercy. It is free from human input. It cannot be nullified. It cannot be postponed. It cannot be explained away! This is Israel's hour of receiving His covenant mercy and kindness.

Some say God chose Abraham and his descendants to be only a temporary representative people on earth, during the long period of the Law until the coming of Jesus who would save the World. Thus, they say, Israel no longer has a claim to the Abrahamic covenant.

It is true Israel no longer has an *exclusive* claim, because Jesus removed the wall of partition and opened the door for the Gentiles, to be partakers of Abraham's blessings. The Church says the new covenant excludes the Jews until after the Church is raptured. This is the error that has kept the Church in Babylonian captivity. Jesus opened the door for the Gentiles to be included. Gentiles have no claim to the Abrahamic blessings, except through Jesus Christ.

The fact that the New Testament presents Old Testament prophecies contradicts any claims that God is finished with Israel, or He has postponed their inclusion to the end of time. Rather, this present dispensation *fulfills* God's covenantal dealings with Israel. The Gentiles are now included, in the commonwealth of Israel.

At the Jerusalem council, the apostles addressed the tension between ceremonial Judaism and Christianity. The Gentiles were not to be forced into the Jewish mold in order to be included in the commonwealth of Israel:

> *"Now the apostles and elders came together to consider this matter. And when there had been much dispute, Peter rose up and said to them: 'Men and brethren, you know that a good while ago God chose among us, that by my mouth the Gentiles should hear the word of the gospel and believe.*
>
> *So God, who knows the heart, acknowledged them by giving them the Holy Spirit, just as He did to us, and made no distinction between us and them, purifying their hearts by faith.*
>
> *Now therefore, why do you test God by putting a yoke on the neck of the disciples which neither our fathers nor we were able to bear?"* **Acts 15:6–10.**
>
> *Therefore I judge that we should not trouble those from among the Gentiles who are turning to God, but that we write to them to abstain from things polluted by idols, from sexual immorality, from things strangled, and from blood."* **Acts 15: 19–20.**

The apostles did not demonize the Mosaic Law but simply said one could not be justified by the Law, but by grace alone. The early Apostolic Church was a Jewish institution, which saw in Jesus of Nazareth the fulfillment of all pertinent promises made to their fathers. They understood that the old order of the Law had been temporary; the permanent had come, thereby *"disannulling of the commandment going before."* Hebrews 7:18.

Jesus, thereby removing the curse of the Law, fulfilled the covenant that God established with Moses. Therefore the Gentile Church is under grace and not the Mosaic Law, as the basis of covenantal relationship, yet the Law remains valid as the holiness standard:

> *"What shall we say then? Is the law sin? Certainly not! On the contrary, I would not have known sin except through the law. For I would not have known covetousness unless the law had said, You shall not covet."* Romans 7:7.
>
> *"For the law of the Spirit of life in Christ Jesus has made me free from the law of sin and death."* Romans 8:2.

The Old Testament sacrifices were a means to maintain the relationship with God in order to appropriate the Abrahamic blessings. The Law was never the basis of the covenant relationship. It was by God's sovereign grace alone that Abraham was chosen to come into the covenant.

The Law was a later addition only as a condition to maintain the blessings. It was to prepare the people for participation in the unconditional blessings given by grace alone. The Law was never meant to justify Israel. The Law cannot justify a sinner; only the blood of an innocent lamb can do that *"and without the shedding of blood is no remission."* Hebrews 9:22.

The Law has no power to sanctify Israel. It was given to *expose* the sin of Israel and the world. Jesus came to *take away* the sins of those, *whosoever will,* among Israel and the Gentiles who repent and accept His offer. As Peter said to the Jews on the day of Pentecost, the promise is to Israel, first, and "to all that are afar off, even as many as the Lord our God shall call." *The Law now describes the new creation in Christ*, defining our new position in Him. It describes Christ's character being reflected in our lives by the in-dwelling Holy Spirit. The blood of Jesus cleanses us from all sin and unrighteousness. Jesus is our righteousness. He is our holiness. He is our justifier. He is our cleanser. He is our blesser. He is our sanctifier.

"Behold, the days are coming, says the LORD, when I will make a new covenant with the house of Israel and with the house of Judah–not according to the covenant that I made with their fathers in the day that I took them by the hand to lead them out of the land of Egypt, My covenant which they broke, though I was a husband to them, says the LORD.

But this is the covenant that I will make with the house of Israel after those days, says the LORD: I will put My law in their minds, and write it on their hearts; and I will be their God, and they shall be My people. No more shall every man teach his neighbor, and every man his brother saying, 'Know the LORD, for they all shall know Me, from the least of them to the greatest of them, says the LORD. For I will forgive their iniquity, and their sin I will remember no more." **Jeremiah 31–34.**

JEWS IN THE DIASPORA – THE DARK AGES

THE TRUTH ABOUT THE DARK AGES

Jewish contributions to world civilization and democracy are without question. It is believed that Christopher Columbus was a Jew who founded the New World for Europe. He paved the way for the persecuted Church to escape to America, in search of religious freedom. Columbus lived in the last years of the Dark Ages, an era of ignorance, in which Jews were scapegoats for the ills of society. The truth of the matter is that anti-Semitists caused the Dark Ages.

During the Dark Ages (476–1492), especially in the period of the Spanish Inquisition, most Jews were accused as heretics, Judaizers and abettors of blasphemers. The Dark Ages were an affliction and a nightmare. During the 14th century plague, called the Black Death, Jews were accused of poisoning the wells. Jews were stripped naked, flogged, hanged, clubbed to death and strangled. They were falsely accused of "blood libel." It was alleged that the Jews sought Christian blood, a practice ascribed to certain pages in the Talmud, though no such pages exist.

This malignant demonizing of the Jewish race was everywhere in the Christian countries of Europe. At the Council of Clermont on November 27, 1095, Pope Urban II issued the first call for a Crusade to liberate Jerusalem. The call ignited the most vicious persecution of Jews in Europe and Palestine. Christians falsely accused Jews of burning the Church of the Holy Sepulcher in Jerusalem.

The event that best crystallized this anti-Jewish sentiment over Europe during the Crusades was in Rouen, a French city under the English crown. Jews were dragged into Church and those who refused baptism were killed.

On May 3, 1096, the Christians attacked the Jews of Speyer, Germany, as they worshiped in the synagogue. The Jews were exterminated and massacred for refusing to be assimilated or converted to Christianity. Later, in the city of Worms, about 800 Jews died at the hands of Christians.

In France, the persecution was also severe. In Troy, in 1147, the Crusaders said to Rabbi Jacob ben Meir, "You are the greatest of men in Israel, therefore we are taking vengeance on you because of him who was hanged (Jesus) and we are going to wound you just as you Jews inflicted five wounds on our God."

King Philip II, in 1182, ordered the expulsion of every Jew out of Christian France. According to one chronicle, Richard of Poitiers, the Crusaders massacred the Jews of all Gaul, except those who converted.

In the preamble to the Fourth Lateran Council in Rome, in 1215, the Church declared the Jews were to be protected because of their special role in the divine plan. St. Augustine urged that Jews should not be forced to convert to Christianity. Jews' corpses were not to be exhumed and defiled. Christians had "no right to kill Jews."

Though this was the right thing for the Church to do, it was short-lived, because the spirit of anti-Semitism was not dealt with totally. The same Council ratified the segregation of Jews from Christians and also decreed that they wear distinctive garments.

Edward I of England later ordered that every Jew seven years old or more wear a yellow taffeta badge above the heart. In Sicily, the emblem was a blue badge in the shape of the letter T.

- In 1290, Edward I expelled the Jews from England.
- In 1492, all Jews were expelled from Spain.

The Jews have been deported, persecuted, dehumanized and debased in the name of Christ. What shall we say about these things?

The dispensation of salvation by grace and faith alone has not shown any grace to the Jews. The history of the Church is stained with the blood of innocent Jews. The Lord is grieved by the persecution of the Jews.

"These six things the LORD hates, Yes, seven are an abomination to Him; A proud look, A lying tongue, Hands that shed innocent blood, A heart that devises wicked plans, Feet that are swift in running to evil, A false witness who

speaks lies, And one who sows discord among brethren."
Proverbs 6:16–19.

The Jews During The Protestant Reformation

In 1523, Martin Luther said regarding Jews, at the beginning of the Reformation: "The Jews are blood relatives, cousins and brothers of our Lord, if His flesh and blood could be boasted of, the Jews belong to Jesus Christ much more than we do. Hence I beg my dear Papists to call me a Jew."

However, the Reformation proved disastrous for European Jews, as the Church resolved to stamp out every heresy, and the Jews were not exempt. In 1553 the Church endorsed the burning of the Talmud. The Reformers tried in vain to win Jews to the Protestant faith. The Jews were trapped between Catholicism and Protestantism.

Martin Luther had reached out to the Jews and opposed the Church's teaching against them. However, Luther failed to persuade them to accept Jesus as their Messiah. In 1543 he turned against them in an inflammatory proclamation titled "Against the Jews and Their Lies." He labeled the Jews thieves and vermin suggesting Jews be deported out of the country. Unfortunately, Martin Luther was a product of his age. He was driven by human indignation when he understood that the Jews were not going to embrace the newfound faith of the great reformer.

Four hundred years later the Nazis reproduced Martin Luther's anti-Jewish writings. In 1935, the Nuremberg laws excommunicated and expelled all Jews from German society. Hitler sought for the final solution to the Jewish question: the Holocaust.

Christendom continued to accuse the Jews and to condemn them as Christ-killers, sucklers of sows, a pariah people, infidels, enemies of the Church. The Church must repent for the sins of the Church Fathers. How long shall we continue to hurt the heart of God by hating His People?

GOD'S LOVE FOR ISRAEL

Ezekiel's Vision of Dry Bones

The prophet Ezekiel predicted the coming glorious resurrection of Israel's Messianic Kingdom.

"Then He said to me, "Son of man, these bones are the whole house of Israel. They indeed say, 'Our bones are dry, our hope is lost, and we ourselves are cut off!' Therefore prophesy and say to them, 'Thus says the LORD GOD: "Behold, O My people, I will open your graves and cause you to come up from your graves, and bring you into the land of Israel. Then you shall know that I am the LORD, when I have opened your graves, O My people, and brought you up from your graves. I will put My Spirit in you, and you shall live, and I will place you in your own land. Then you shall know that I, the LORD, have spoken it and performed it.' Says the LORD." **Ezekiel 37:11–14.**

Ezekiel's vision makes it evident that Israel would go through a period of deadness. The Gentile Church sees the dry bones and criticizes them for dying. The Church blames them! Kicks them! Ridicules them! Despises them! Throws them away! Hates them!

The wonder of divine love and compassion is God's faithfulness to His Ancient People, in spite of themselves. He will breathe life into them and raise them up as a mighty army. The Church should stop hating Israel. God commands the Church today to change its message to one of love and acceptance, even as the word says:

"Comfort, yes, comfort My people!" Says your God. "Speak comfort to Jerusalem, and cry out to her, That her warfare is ended, That her iniquity is pardoned; For she has received from the LORD's hand double for all her sins." **Isaiah 40:1–2.**

Lazarus – A Symbol of Israel

A story in the Gospel that dramatizes Israel's relationship with God is the death and resurrection of Lazarus. Lazarus, who was precious to Jesus, died and was buried four days. Then Jesus raised him from the dead. Their relationship parallels God's covenant bond with Abraham, the friend of God. Jesus wept for Lazarus, overcome by His emotion, for a friend He deeply loved.

Jesus also wept for Jerusalem. How much God loves Israel! Though she may be spiritually dead she remains beloved of God.

The Prodigal Son

The prodigal son is a type and shadow of the Gentile people. The elder brother is Israel. The early Jewish Church had problems with Gentiles saved without circumcision, received by God and given the gift of the Holy Spirit. Like the elder brother, the Jewish people have been working for God for two thousand years without a party. They were laboring under the beggarly elements of the Law. The Gentiles came and they received mercy and grace from God the Father. The Jews think salvation by grace alone is cheap and not Biblical. It is hard for them to rejoice with Gentiles coming in so cheaply.

The Unforgiving Servant

To recall another parable–the Gentile Church is the servant who owed the King tens of thousands of talents and was forgiven by the King, yet he cannot forgive his fellow servant Israel who owes him a few hundred dollars.

"But that servant went out and found one of his fellow servants who owed him a hundred denarii; and he laid hands on him and took him by the throat, saying, 'Pay me what you owe!' So his fellow servant fell down at his feet and begged him saying, 'Have patience with me, and I will pay you all.' And he would not, but went and threw him into prison till he should pay the debt." **Matthew 18:28–30.**

The future of "the rejectionists and replacementists" is clearly outlined in this parable, whose fulfillment is imminent. The Church is guilty of its hostility to Israel.

"So when his fellow servants saw what had been done, they were very grieved, and came and told their master all that had been done. Then his master, after he had called him, said to him, 'You wicked servant! I forgave you all that debt because you begged me. Should you not also have had compassion on your fellow servant, just as I had pity on you?' And his master was angry, and delivered him to the torturers until he should pay all that was due to him.

So my heavenly Father also will do to you if each of you,
from his heart, does not forgive his brother his trespasses."
Matthew 18: 31–35.

If the Church does not repent it will be given over to tormentors. The Church is holding the Jews in jail, isolated, rejected, persecuted and hated.

Joseph's Brothers

In the Book of Genesis, it is unquestionable that Joseph typified Israel, elected and exalted by the Father, and hated by his Gentile brothers. As Joseph's brothers tried to destroy him, so have the Gentiles tried to destroy Israel in vain. The sovereignty of God preserved Israel in the Diaspora, in the wilderness of nations, against the will of the Gentile Church committed to destroying all the Jews. The existence of Israel is a testimony to God's faithfulness to the covenant that He made with Abraham.

Here we have a phenomenon that even the adherents of rejection and *replacement theology* cannot deny: God's abiding love for Israel, in spite of her sin. This is doubly made clear by the fact that she has been gathered back to her ancient land of promise after nearly two thousand years in dispersion. Israel is the apple of God's eye, the supreme example of His controlling and directing influence upon the affairs of humankind. All things are moving toward His eternal purpose to establish on earth a Messianic Kingdom and restore Israel unto Himself.

Haman's Plot

Once more we revert to the history of Israel in the Gentile world. In the book of Esther, we are told the reason for the Jewish feast of Purim. It is a reminder of the faithfulness of God on behalf of His people, Israel, against Gentile efforts to wipe them out. As Haman conspired to kill every Jew in the world, so have Jews through the centuries been marked for destruction or extermination.

This is another illustration of how Satan wants to accuse Jews in the common house of humankind and destroy them. This event foreshadowed Israel's experience in the age of the Gentiles. This was a prophecy about the Church. Esther is a type of the true Church, in the royal palace seated together with Christ, and pleading for natural Israel. Haman represents the self-righteous, proud, and arrogant

Gentile, apostate Church that hates Israel. Israel has a kinsman redeemer in heaven, Jesus of Nazareth—the Messiah of Israel.

Modern Hamans claim God has replaced Israel with the Church. They maintain that God is punishing Israel for rejecting and crucifying God's Son. Scriptures are clear that *our sins* killed Him, and that He died according to the Scriptures or by the determinate will of God preordained before the foundation of the world.

Even if the Jews are guilty of betraying Jesus to be crucified by the Gentiles, Jesus prayed: *"Father, forgive them, for they do not know what they do."* Luke 23:34. The only people that find it hard to forgive them are the Gentiles. When God forgives, He forgets. He is not holding the Jews responsible for His Son's blood. Every person on Earth is responsible. He died for our sins. He is our substitute. He is the Lamb of God, slain for the sins of the whole world.

THE ISSUE OF JEWISH BLINDNESS

There is also confusion over the issue of Jewish blindness that Paul talks about in Chapter 11 of Romans. Jewish blindness does not mean Jewish exclusion. It is a partial blindness. The Gospel is for "whosoever will," both Jew and Gentile. There is no Biblical basis for the Church's prejudices–anti-Semitism camouflaged by false theological trappings. Our thoughts are not His thoughts. Israel is still beloved of God. They remain God's top priority in this age of grace.

> *"What then? Israel has not obtained what it seeks; but the elect have obtained it, and the rest were blinded. Just as it is written:*
>
> *"God has given them a spirit of stupor,*
> *Eyes that they should not see*
> *And ears that they should not hear,*
> *To this very day."*
>
> *And David says:*
>
> *"Let their table become a snare and a trap,*
> *A stumbling block and a recompense to them,*
> *Let their eyes be darkened, so that they do not see,*
> *And bow down their back always."* **Romans 11:7–10.**

This is a passage *replacement theology* interpreted to mean that God is completely through with the Jews. The blindness of Israel is partial and judicial– never complete and final. God has yet to fulfill all of His promises to the nation of Israel. It is amazing how these "de-judaizing expositors" choose which passage to apply to natural Israel and which ones to the so called spiritual Israel–the Church. Usually the judgment passages are for literal Israel and the blessed promises for the Church.

The remnant is the elect among the Jewish people throughout the ages and the blinded part is the unbelieving apostate that Isaiah spoke about.

> *"For the LORD has poured out on you the Spirit of deep sleep,*
> *And has closed your eyes, namely, the prophets;*
> *And He has covered your heads, namely, the seers."* Isaiah 29:10.

God has put a deep sleep upon Israel. He will wake her up at the appointed time. The revelation of Jesus as the suffering servant of God—their Messiah—has been sealed to them. The prophets and apostles predicted and outlined Israel's history.

Israel has zeal after God without knowledge. Her rebellion is curable and all Israel will be saved. Whereas, the Gentile apostate Church will be cut off forever, because though they had the knowledge of God, they had no zeal or fear of God. They have the form, but deny the power thereof. 2 Timothy 3:5.

God is making one new creation of Jew and Gentile, one flock. He's one Shepherd, one Father of us all! The Church is blinded by *replacement theology,* therefore a candidate of the apostasy and the falling away predicted by the Apostle Paul in 2 Thessalonians chapter 2.

The crux of the matter is the integrity of God and His faithfulness to His unfaithful people. Every Jew is not blinded. Jews have been saved all through the centuries.

The most critical and significant fact is the permanence of Israel's place in God's economy. *Israel is central to God's purposes today.* God has not marginalized Israel's role during the times of the Gentiles, though the Church has done so.

PHARISAIC JUDAISM'S LOSS OF FAITH

The error of Judaism was replacing the faith of Abraham with "the traditions of men." The Jews sought to earn their position of privilege by outward performance. God required of Israel an attitude of worship in spirit and truth, not works; yet, throughout the ages, they continued to choose religion rather than relationship.

David was a man after God's own heart. He had caught the vision of high praises. He worshiped the Father. He walked with God. He knew that everything was a gift of God by grace alone.

How could performance earn for Israel what God had already given them, in the eternal covenant He cut with Abraham? Election is always a sovereign work of God. It is always by grace alone. Israel still today is chosen by grace alone.

National blessings belong to the natural Israel forever. The Promised Land belongs to them forever. There is no power on earth that can give it away in any peace agreement or United Nations resolutions.

Israel was preserved in Egypt and delivered from slavery, because of the Abrahamic covenant, not because she was good and was keeping the Law. God is faithful to His covenant in spite of us. Moses said to Israel:

"The LORD did not set His love on you nor choose you because you were more than any other people, for you were the least of all peoples; but because the LORD loves you, and because He would keep the oath which He swore to your fathers, the LORD has brought you out with a mighty hand, and redeemed you from the house of bondage, from the hand of Pharaoh king of Egypt.

Therefore know that the LORD your God, He is God, the faithful God who keeps covenant and mercy for a thousand generations with those who love Him and keep His commandments; and He repays those who hate Him to their face, to destroy them. He will not be slack with him who hates Him; He will repay him to his face. Therefore you shall keep the commandments, the statutes, and the judgments which I command you today, to observe them.

Then it shall come to pass, because you listen to these judgment, and keep and do them, that the LORD your God will keep with you the covenant and the mercy which He swore to your fathers." **Deuteronomy 7:7–12.**

God is still faithful to Israel because of His covenant with Abraham. He is still the God of Abraham, Isaac and Jacob. He is the Holy One of Israel! He still has a plan for Israel. God gave Jesus of Nazareth all power in heaven, on Earth and under the Earth, as the Son of David. He will save Israel. Paul says:

"And so all Israel will be saved, as it is written:

"The Deliverer will come out of Zion,
And He will turn away ungodliness from Jacob;For this is
My covenant with them,
When I take away their sins." **Romans 11:26.**

Anti-Semitism Today and The Kairos Hour of Repentance

Mark well the unconditionality of the Abrahamic covenant, which is delivered without obscurity or ambiguity. We must stand only on the authority of the Scriptures. The Church has been behind most of Israel's suffering throughout the Christian Age. The Lord commands His saints to separate themselves from the whore that compromises His word. The whore Church hates Israel. She pays lip service; she is arrogant. She is self- seeking and self-serving. She has no budgetary consideration to show mercy to the Jewish People. God is going to cast her out. God is separating the Bride, Blood-washed, Bible-believing, Spirit- led, Jew-loving remnant.

> *"And I heard another voice from heaven saying, "Come out of her, my people lest you share in her sins, and lest you receive of her plagues. For her sins have reached to heaven and God has remembered her iniquities. Render to her just as she rendered to you, and repay her double according to her works; in the cup which she has mixed, mix double for her."* **Revelation 18: 4–6.**

Anti-Semitism is a *rational* deduction of the historicity of Jesus' earthly ministry. *Revelation* sees in the same events the Father's heart of abiding love for Israel. Though her house was made desolate, yet her spiritual Kingdom was established in preparation for the Messianic Kingdom at His Second Coming. The Father scattered Israel into the wilderness of nations, where the Church could have shown mercy to her. What a glorious opportunity for those who were once "no people" and who now have become the people of God, kings and priests unto the God of Abraham! However, the Church abused the privilege for two thousand years.

Anti-Semitism is *legalism*. When we reflect upon the motive, it is clear that we accept grace for ourselves, but law for the Jews. The Jewish people are under obligation to fulfill all the law, while we come in through grace. We justify their condition as a judgment of God. This double standard we apply suggests that Jesus did not die for their sins, but for only the Gentiles' sin. Thus it becomes almost equivalent to blasphemy of the Holy Spirit.

Anti-Semitism is a curse on the Church. One of the worst travesties of Christianity is people who profess that they are children of God but do not express the love of God's children. We regard Jews as the paradigm of evil. It is evident in our theology how much we disdain and disregard Jews. We have made them into an abject lesson.

Oh, how much we disgrace the name of the Lord when we fail to walk in love. How can we love God and hate His own brethren? John tells us clearly that we cannot love God and hate our brothers. We are both children of Abraham.

> *"If someone says, "I love God," and hates his brother, he is a liar; for he who does not love his brother whom he has seen, how can he love God whom he has not seen? And this commandment we have from Him: that he who loves God must love his brother also."* 1 John 4:20-21.

This is the *kairos*, 'the appointed time' - for the Church to repent for hating Her brethren, children of Abraham, fellow citizens and joint heirs of the Abrahamic covenant. The Church can no longer ignore the Jewish issue.

Compromise of the word always produces confusion.

> *"Remember therefore from where you have fallen; repent and do the first works, or else I will come to you quickly and remove your lampstand from its place – unless you repent."* Revelation 2:5.

The authoritative and infallible Word of God acknowledges the existence of a presumptuous people, who deny "that the callings of God are without repentance" and that "God is not a man that He would lie." The Apostle John, the writer of the Book of Revelation, addresses these arrogant and proud people who claim to be Jews but are not. This is what he says regarding them:

> *"Indeed I will make those of the synagogue of Satan, who say they are Jews and are not, but lie – indeed I will make them come and worship before your feet, and to know that I have loved you."* Revelation 3:9.

"I know your works, tribulation, and poverty (but you are rich); and I know the blasphemy of those who say they are Jews and are not, but are a synagogue of Satan." Revelation 2:9.

The Word of God calls the *replacement of Israel* with the Gentiles, "blasphemy of them which say they are Jews and *are not* but are the synagogue of *Satan*." The "synagogue of Satan" includes non-Jews who claim to be the new Israel, having only the form of godliness but denying the power thereof. Satan is the one who wants the Jews cut off forever, so he can accuse God of not keeping His promise to Abraham, Isaac, and Jacob.

Here is the only answer to the Jewish issue: repentance and development of a becoming attitude of godly fear and praise for Him, the only Wise God, who keeps His covenant to a thousand generations. Bible-believing and God-loving Christians cannot hate God's Chosen People. Anti-Semitism did not exist in the New Testament Church which was Jewish. It developed after the Apostles died and continues as a pernicious cancer to this day.

In the final analysis the issue is, "Who killed Jesus—the Jews, or your sins and my sin?" Did Jesus die according to "the plan of man, or the plan of God?" How is it that the cross, the symbol of love and redemption, has become the instrument of death to the Jews?

God was in Christ reconciling the world to Himself through the tragedy of the cross, that all might be saved, Jew and Gentile. Yet, the Gentile Church has persecuted the Jewish people, in the name of Jesus Christ. He died according to the will of God and not the will of people. Jews did not kill Jesus. Our sins killed Him. The Jews do not need us. We need them to be grafted into the glorious Kingdom of God.

THE NEW CREATION – JEW AND GENTILE

There are only two groups of people, two Kingdoms: the Kingdom of Light and the Kingdom of Darkness; the new creation and the old creation; the seed of the first Adam and the seed of the second Adam. *The new humanity has neither distinctions nor standards.* Galatians 3:28, 1 Corinthians 7:19.

> *"...There is neither Greek nor Jew, circumcised nor uncircumcised, barbarian, Scythian, slave nor free, but Christ is all and in all."* Colossians 3:11.

The "one new man" is the community of God's elect on Earth, a full realization of history and Abraham's covenant. This new creation consummates God's Old Testament dealings, to call out a people unto Himself from all the families of the Earth, to enjoy the Abrahamic covenant of blessings - to bring near those who were afar off. God has made in Christ–one new man of both Jew and Gentile, one flock, one people, with one Lord and Savior.

These "ecclesia," (the *called out ones*) walk contrary to the world. They are a Kingdom people. They are in the world, but not of the world. They are citizens of Heaven. They are born from above. However, let us not be mistaken: all Israel is not the *Israel of God*, and all the Church is not the *Church of God.* Those who are walking according to this present world are not His, whether Jew or Gentile.

The Mystery of the Ages

The inclusion of Gentiles into the Commonwealth of Israel was a mystery hidden to the Jews. The mystery is not that Jews are replaced by the Church as God's elect, as the Church later taught. It is the unfolding of God's plan to make Jew and Gentile one in Christ and joint heirs of the Abrahamic covenant as Paul says to the Colossians:

*"I now rejoice in my sufferings for you, and fill up in my
flesh what is lacking in the afflictions of Christ, for the sake
of His body, which is the church, of which I became a
minister according to the stewardship from God which was
given to me for you, to fulfill the word of God, the mystery
which has been hidden from ages and from generations but
now has been revealed to His saints. To them God willed to
make known what are the riches of the glory of this mystery
among the Gentiles: which is Christ in you, the hope of
glory. "* **Colossians 1:24–27.**

The Jews did not realize that the Kingdom would come in two
stages. The first advent of the Messiah would initiate the phase of the
Kingdom as a spiritual reality. The Church, Jew and Gentile, is a
prelude to the physical manifestation of the Kingdom at the Second
Coming.

God is creating a new humanity in the person of Jesus, a new
history–indeed a new Kingdom. The humanity is neither Jew nor
Gentile. It is a new reality on Earth.

The Jewish people expected an earthly Messiah and the triumph
of good over evil on earth, when the Messiah would rule over all
humankind and integrate all creation into His plan of the ages. Instead,
Jesus came to call out of every language and nation a people unto
Himself, generations of men and women, who have received the
revelation "thou art the Christ, the son of the living God," to become
His spiritual Kingdom today.

Jesus Christ, a Jew, Son of David, came to create "the Israel of
God" from both Jew and Gentile. He accomplished perfect
redemption. He removed the wall of partition and made the two, one in
Him.

*"For there is no distinction between Jew and Greek, for the
same Lord over all is rich to all who call upon Him, For
"whosoever calls on the name of the LORD shall be saved."*
Romans 10:12–13.

A believer is a citizen of the commonwealth of Israel. Jesus, who
universalized the Abrahamic covenantal blessings, brought in the
once-alien Gentiles.

*"That at that time you were without Christ, being aliens
from the commonwealth of Israel and strangers from the*

covenants of promise, having no hope and without God in the world. But now in Christ Jesus you who once were far off have been brought near by the blood of Christ.

For He Himself is our peace, who has made both one, and has broken down the middle wall of separation, having abolished in His flesh the enmity, that is, the law of commandments contained in ordinances, so as to create in Himself one new man from the two, thus making peace, and that He might reconcile them both to God in one body through the cross, thereby putting to death the enmity." **Ephesians 2:12–15.**

The Gospel's Message of Love to Both Jew and Gentile

God planned everything that happened to Jesus, in order to redeem humankind. God's Kingdom plan is on course. The Kingdom came as a mustard seed, and now it covers the whole world. Jesus is King today, ruling in the hearts of His people. The will of God is being done on Earth as it is in Heaven. Israel's final destiny yet to be fulfilled.

There is a large part of the body of Christ that teaches the *two-people* theory. One, being an Earthly people that are natural Israel and second, being a heavenly people, who are the spiritual Israel, called the Church. Does the Bible teach us dual salvation and two programs? It teaches one salvation, through Jesus of Nazareth and one destiny, of Jew and Gentile.

The only way we can come to understand the mystery of Christ and the Church is to understand the mystery of Israel and the Church. The Gospel narrative is rooted in the story of Israel. The New Testament continues displaying the divine design of God's purposes for Israel. Our fundamental responsibility to the Jewish people is to make them jealous as we lay down our lives for them. The salvation of Jews is riches to the Gentiles.

"Now if their fall is riches for the world, and their failure riches for the Gentiles, how much more their fullness!" Romans 11:12.

The times of the Gentiles will come to an end, when the fullness of the Gentiles has come.

> *"But the Scripture has confined all under sin, that the promise by faith in Jesus Christ might be given to those who believe."* **Galatians 3:22.**

God included all, Jew and Gentile, under sin. No flesh is justified before God, *"for all have sinned, and come short of the glory of God."* Romans 3:23. Duality of covenants teaches that Jews can attain righteousness under the Law, when Scripture is clear that the Law can justify no flesh.

"Now a mediator does not mediate for one only." Galatians 3:20.

The Law cannot justify the sinner. The Law demands justice. The holiness of God demands punishment of sin. The wages of sin is death. The Scriptures never taught duality. Jesus did not teach duality. The Apostles did not teach duality. Jesus spoke of making one flock of Jews and Gentiles. The Apostles established one Church of Jews and Gentiles.

> *"For you are all sons of God through faith in Christ Jesus. For as many of you as were baptized into Christ have put on Christ. There is neither Jew nor Greek, there is neither slave nor free, there is neither male nor female; for you are all one in Christ Jesus. And if you are Christ's then you are Abraham's seed, and heirs according to the promise."* **Galatians 3:26–29.**

ISRAEL'S FINAL DESTINY

JERUSALEM

What is the final destiny? Global economic collapse, food shortages, pandemics, biological warfare, blood red moons, a black sun, nuclear holocaust and unprecedented natural disasters. A nightmarish landscape you need to escape.

The world is on the brink of terminal catastrophe–the battle of Armageddon for Eretz Israel. The present peace talks violate the Holy Covenant and are a roadmap to doomsday. The two-state solution, which partitions the Holy Land puts humankind on a collision course with the Holy One of Israel. He said He will bring back the children of Israel to restore the ancient places in the last days.

Eretz Israel is a sacred and holy precinct on earth. God clearly declares in the Torah, *"the land is mine."* Leviticus 25:23. Canaan is Yahweh's land grant to Abraham's descendants. He specifically gave it to Isaac's seed in an eternal covenant.

"I give to you and your descendants after you the land in which you are a stranger, all the land of Canaan, as an everlasting possession; and I will be their God." **Genesis 17:8.**

Eretz Israel is the geographical platform for the endgame. It is a special land where God has enacted the greatest events including the incarnation, birth, death, burial and resurrection of Jesus Christ. He ascended back to Heaven from Jerusalem. He promised to return and establish His Millennium Kingdom in Israel.

The land granted to Abraham was occupied by the Canaanites, Hittites, Amorites, Perizzites, Hivites and Jebusites. It was always occupied land. The territory has been in dispute since the beginning. God dispossessed the indigenous people groups 400 years after their cup of iniquity was full.

"Then He said to Abram: "Know certainly that your descendants will be strangers in a land that is not theirs,

*and will serve them, and they will afflict them four hundred
years. And also the nation whom they serve I will judge;
afterward they shall come out with great possessions. Now
as for you, you shall go to your fathers in peace; you shall
be buried at a good old age. But in the fourth generation
they shall return here, for the iniquity of the Amorites is not
yet complete."* **Genesis 15:13–16.**

Israel's journey to its manifest destiny began in a place called
Ur in Mesopotamia, where God called Abraham to leave and go to a
land He would show him. We are approaching Israel's final
destination–a journey through the centuries: From the Exodus, the
return from Babylonian exile, the destruction of the First and Second
Temples, the Diaspora, the persecutions, pogroms, holocausts, the
divine preservation, the rebirth and formation of the modern state of
Israel. And finally, the return of Israel's Messiah.

In this context, it should be clear why the Jews are viewed as
enemies of humankind. It's because of Western replacement theology
and Islamic dogma that claims that Ishmael was chosen and not Isaac.

Sad to say, all of this anti-Semitism was built up by Christendom.
Han Kung is correct in his accusation of the Church:

"Nazi Anti-Judaism was the work of godless Anti-Christian
criminals...but without the almost two thousand year-long history of
Christian Anti-Judaism... it would not have been possible... None of
the anti-Jewish measures of the Nazi...distinctive clothing, exclusion
from professions, forbidding of mixed marriages, expulsions, the
concentration camps, massacres, gruesome funeral pyres was new. All
that already existed in so-called Christian Middle Ages... and in the
period of the Christian Reformation."

What makes things even more complicated is that the Jews in
Eretz Israel are split between "the peace nicks and the conservatives"
who reject the idea of giving away God's land for a promised peace.
There are also two groups among the Arabs. The moderate Arab
nations want land for peace and the radical Arab nations reject land for
peace. They want Israel wiped out off the map. The Church is divided.
The majority of Christendom wants to see land for peace talks end
successfully, and a minority believes in the Holy Covenant and rejects
land for peace. What about the rest of the world? They just want an
end to global terrorism and undisrupted oil supply from the Arab
nations.

THE ROAD TO JERUSALEM: ISRAEL'S ETERNAL CAPITAL

The rebirth of the modern state of Israel sets the stage for the final battle on earth. The word "Armageddon" is compounded from the Hebrew "Har-Megiddo" –the Hill of Megiddo. The Hill of Megiddo overlooks the valley of Jezreel. Many historical battles have been fought in this valley. Napoleon Bonaparte standing on Har Megiddo said: "All the armies in the world could fight here."

All the armies of the world will be gathered in Israel to wipe out the Jews from the face of the earth in that valley. Land for peace talks are going to lead to false peace and to the greatest gathering of the armies of the world since the dawn of time. As Israel's existence lies in the balance, the building of the third Temple on Temple Mount will begin to take on a larger and larger reality.

Caliph el Malik built the Dome of the Rock, 70 years after Mohammad's death and 60 years after Arab conquest of Jerusalem. He took it without a struggle. The Byzantine Patriarch Sophronius surrendered the city to Umayyad Caliph Umar Omar Ibn Al Khattab in 638 AD. During Byzantine rule, Temple Mount was turned into the city garbage dump. The Muslims cleared up the dump and found the rock where Abraham prepared the altar to offer up his son Isaac. They built the Dome of the Rock on the Qubbat Al Sakhra. Today, Temple Mount has proven to be the most sensitive issue in the peace negotiations as both Judaism and Islam want exclusive rights.

The Church needs to avoid its mistake when the Third Reich attempted to wipe out the Jews from the face of the earth. Christendom remained silent. The Church needs to learn from its past mistakes and rethink its recent past. The rebirth of Israel as a nation in her ancient homeland as predicted by the prophets of old should be proof enough that God is keeping His covenant with Israel.

It is important to realize that since the promises in the Torah are given to a literal descendant of Jacob, they will literally be fulfilled to Israel.

Historically no less than 96 church councils and 114 Popes declared edicts against the Jews treating them as pariah people and condoning and encouraging their unimaginable suffering at the hands of Christian civilization.

Jerusalem is mentioned 656 times in the Old Testament and 139 times in the New Testament. It was a Jebusite city that David captured. It became known by many names, City of David, Zion, City of the

Great King, Holy City and The Holy Mountain. God chose to put His name there forever.

"I have chosen Jerusalem, that My name may be there, and I have chosen David to be over My people Israel." 2 Chronicles 6:6.

Since God chose Jerusalem it has been conquered 37 times and has changed hands 86 times. Jerusalem has always been ground zero in the Middle East conflict. All through the centuries the great empires of the world have fought to control it: Nebuchadnezzar, Pompey, Godfred of Bouillon, Saladin, Crusaders, General Allenby. General Moshe Dyan liberated East Jerusalem and Temple Mount in the 6-Day War in 1967.

In Hebrew the name Jerusalem means 'the foundation of peace'. There will not be peace on earth until the Prince of Peace rules from Jerusalem. The Glory of God will return to Jerusalem and fill the Third Temple. The prophet Ezekiel previewed the coming Glory of God to His Temple in Jerusalem in our generation:

"Afterward he brought me to the gate, the gate that faces toward the east. And behold, the glory of the God of Israel came from the way of the east. His voice was like the sound of many waters; and the earth shone with His glory. It was like the appearance of the vision which I saw—like the vision which I saw when I came to destroy the city. The visions were like the vision which I saw by the River Chebar; and I fell on my face. And the glory of the LORD came into the temple by way of the gate which faces toward the east. The Spirit lifted me up and brought me into the inner court; and behold, the glory of the LORD filled the temple. Then I heard Him speaking to me from the temple, while a man stood beside me." **Ezekiel 43: 1–6.**

Ezekiel tells us the exact location on Temple Mount where the Third Temple will be built. This gives us the prime clue that this Temple will exist prior to the end of days. Ezekiel saw a protective wall round about it separating the Third Temple from the profane thing (Dome of the Rock).

"Now when he had finished measuring the inner temple, he brought me out through the gateway that faces toward the east, and measured it all around. He measured the east side

with the measuring rod five hundred rods by the measuring rod all around. He measured the north side, five hundred rods by the measuring rod all around. He measured the south side, five hundred rods by the measuring rod. He came around to the west side and measured five hundred rods by the measuring rod. He measured it on the four sides; it had a wall all around, five hundred cubits long and five hundred wide, to separate the holy areas from the profane thing." Ezekiel 42: 15-20.

The fourth Temple from heaven will not have a wall to separate it from the profane thing, because there will be nothing profane in the New Jerusalem. Ezekiel's vision of the coming glory is of the Third Temple that the Jews are getting ready to build.

THE BATTLE OF ARMAGEDDON

Every journey has a point of origin and termination. Armageddon will be the war to end all wars. It will cover 1600 furlongs or two hundred miles, the length of Palestine today. Think about it, this battlefield will encompass the whole land from the North–Valley of Megiddo to the Central–Valley of Jehoshaphat ending in the South in Ancient Edom.

"And I saw three unclean spirits like frogs coming out of the mouth of the dragon, out of the mouth of the beast, and out of the mouth of the false prophet. For they are spirits of demons, performing signs, which go out to the kings of the earth and of the whole world, to gather them to the battle of that great day of God Almighty.

"Behold, I am coming as a thief. Blessed is he who watches, and keeps his garments, lest he walk naked and they see his shame." And they gathered them together to the place called in Hebrew, Armageddon. Then the seventh angel poured out his bowl into the air, and a loud voice came out of the temple of heaven, from the throne, saying, "It is done!"

And there were noises and thunderings and lightnings; and there was a great earthquake, such a mighty and great earthquake as had not occurred since men were on the earth. Now the great city was divided into three parts, and the cities of the nations fell. And great Babylon was remembered before

God, to give her the cup of the wine of the fierceness of His wrath. Then every island fled away, and the mountains were not found. And great hail from heaven fell upon men, each hailstone about the weight of a talent. Men blasphemed God because of the plague of the hail, since that plague was exceedingly great." **Revelation 16: 13–21.**

The Antichrist as the head of the New World Order will mobilize the NATO power bloc, the Russian Confederacy, the Oriental Power block and the Southern Confederacy, the entire world. The number of the army from the East alone will be 200 million. John in the book of Revelation gives us this preview of that ominous battle.

"And the winepress was trampled outside the city, and blood came out of the winepress, up to the horses' bridles, for one thousand six hundred furlongs." Revelation 14:20.

There will be a river of blood as high as the horse's bridle two hundred miles long!

The emerging New World Order will be obsessed with a single passion to destroy all the Jews and those who support them. The vision of most of the end time battle of Armageddon carries many characteristics of nuclear holocaust, earth splitting explosions, hailstone, brimstone and fire.

"Then the LORD will go forth And fight against those nations, as He fights in the day of battle. And in that day His feet will stand on the Mount of Olives, Which faces Jerusalem on the east. And the Mount of Olives shall be split in two, from east to west, Making a very large valley; Half of the mountain shall move toward the north And half of it toward the south.

And this shall be the plague with which the LORD will strike all the people who fought against Jerusalem:

Their flesh shall dissolve while they stand on their feet, their eyes shall dissolve in their sockets, and their tongues shall dissolve in their mouths." Zechariah 14: 3-4,12.

This is a description of the way it is going to be. This generation is careening headlong into final, cosmic, cataclysmic events without a warning. I am sounding the alarm.

"Blow the trumpet in Zion, And sound an alarm in My holy mountain! Let all the inhabitants of the land tremble; For the day of the LORD is coming, For it is at hand: A day of darkness and gloominess, A day of clouds and thick darkness, Like the morning clouds spread over the mountains. A people come, great and strong, the like of whom has never been; Nor will there ever be any such after them, Even for many successive generations." Joel 2: 1-2.

These are perilous times. The nations of the world are coming into an end time alignment. The world stage is being set by the New World Order to usher in the Antichrist to deceive the world into the final holocaust.

Anti-Semitism is going to reach its zenith in our days, as the Jews will be blamed for the global economic collapse and the Middle East conflict. There will be no help for the Jews except from the Holy One of Israel. This will be the darkest hour for the modern state of Israel, as it stands alone facing imminent extermination.

The Antichrist will sit in the Third Temple blaspheming God and exalting himself as the manifest god in the flesh, the Messiah of Israel, demanding universal worship. He will behead millions of saints who refuse to worship him and take his number 666.

When Israel realizes she has none to help her on earth she will look up to God for help. Suddenly Christ will split the heavens open and descend riding on a white horse, and the host of heaven following him. He will destroy the armies of the world gathered to destroy the Jews with the sword out of his mouth.

"Now I saw heaven opened, and behold, a white horse. And He who sat on him was called Faithful and True, and in righteousness He judges and makes war. His eyes were like a flame of fire, and on His head were many crowns. He had a name written that no one knew except Himself. He was clothed with a robe dipped in blood, and His name is called The Word of God. And the armies in heaven, clothed in fine linen, white and clean followed Him on white horses. Now out of His mouth goes a sharp sword, that with it He should strike the nations. And He Himself will rule them with a rod of iron. He Himself treads the winepress of the fierceness and wrath of Almighty God. And He has on His robe and on His thigh a name written: KING OF KINGS AND LORD OF LORDS.

Then I saw an angel standing in the sun; and he cried with a loud voice, saying to all the birds that fly in the midst of heaven, "Come and gather together for the supper of the great God that you may eat the flesh of kings, the flesh of captains, the flesh of mighty men, the flesh of horses and of those who sit on them, and the flesh of all people, free and slave, both small and great."

And I saw the beast, the kings of the earth, and their armies, gathered together to make war against Him who sat on the horse and against His army. Then the beast was captured, and with him the false prophet who worked signs in his presence, by which he deceived those who received the mark of the beast and those who worshiped his image. These two were cast alive into the lake of fire burning with brimstone. And the rest were killed with the sword which proceeded from the mouth of Him who sat on the horse. And all the birds were filled with their flesh." **Revelation 19: 11–2.**

The manifest destiny of Israel is the glorious coming of her Messiah to save her at her hour of terminal crisis. Christ's eyes will flash with vengeance and the whole world will mourn as He judges righteously those that slaughtered His people. His cloth will be stained with blood of the enemies of the apple of His eye, Israel. This is how Isaiah describes the advent of the Messiah during the offset to the battle of Armageddon.

"Who is this who comes from Edom, with dyed garments from Bozrah, This One who is glorious in His apparel, traveling in the greatness of His strength?— " I who speak in righteousness, mighty to save." Why is Your apparel red, and Your garments like one who treads in the winepress? " I have trodden the winepress alone, and from the peoples no one was with Me. For I have trodden them in My anger, and trampled them in My fury; Their blood is sprinkled upon My garments, and I have stained all My robes. For the day of vengeance is in My heart, and the year of My redeemed has come.

I looked, but there was no one to help, and I wondered that there was no one to uphold; Therefore My own arm brought salvation for Me; And My own fury, it sustained Me. I have trodden down the peoples in My anger, Made them drunk in

My fury, And brought down their strength to the earth, and with blood of the enemies of the apple of His eye, Israel." **Isaiah 63: 1–6.**

As we can see, the providential model of history has a beginning and an end. The careful study of the Jewish story through the centuries will clearly show you need to stand on the right side– the winning side.

TOP TEN REASONS TO STAND WITH ISRAEL

1. **God says He will bless those who bless Israel:**" I will bless those who bless you, and I will curse him who curses you; and in you all the families of the earth shall be blessed." Genesis 12:3.

2. **God says we are to "Comfort" Israel:**" "Comfort, yes, comfort My people! Says your God."Isaiah 40:1.

3. **God says His gifts and call on Israel have not been revoked**: "Concerning the gospel *they are* enemies for your sake, but concerning the election *they are* beloved for the sake of the fathers." Romans 11:28.

4. **God says we owe Israel a debt for the blessings we have received through them**: "You worship what you do not know; we know what we worship, for salvation is of the Jews." John 4:22. "It pleased them indeed, and they are their debtors. For if the Gentiles have been partakers of their spiritual things, their duty is also to minister to them in material things." Romans 15:27.

5. **God says He will bring them back to their land:** "Thus says the Lord GOD: Behold, I will lift My hand in an oath to the Gentiles … They shall bring your sons in *their* arms, And your daughters shall be carried on *their* shoulders." Isaiah 49:22.

6. **God says the Good News is for the Jew first:** "For I am not ashamed of the gospel of Christ for it is the power of God to salvation for everyone who believes, for the Jew first and also to the Gentiles." Romans 1:16.

7. **God says we are one in Christ and fellow heirs:** "For He (Messiah) is our peace, who has made us (Jew & Gentile) both one, and has broken down the dividing wall of hostility…that He might create in Himself one new man in place of the two…making Gentile believers fellow heirs with Israel." Ephesians 2: 14–15, 3:6.

8. **God says Pray for the Peace of Jerusalem:** "Pray for the peace of Jerusalem: they shall prosper that love thee." Psalm 122:6.

9. **God says Israel is precious to Him**: "For he that touches Israel touches the apple of God's eye." Zechariah 2:8.

10. **God says He will raise up intercessors:** "I have posted watchmen on your walls, O Jerusalem; they will never be silent day or night and give Him no rest till He establishes Jerusalem and makes her the praise of the earth." Isaiah 62: 6,7.

TOP TEN REASONS WHY CHRISTIANS SHOULD NOT SUPPORT "LAND FOR PEACE"

1. **God warns the nations not to partition Israel**: "I will also gather all nations…and will plead with them there for my people and for my heritage Israel, whom they have scattered among the nations, and parted my land." Joel 3:2.

2. **God personally owns the Holy Land:** "The land shall not be sold for ever: for the land is Mine; for ye are strangers and sojourners with Me." Leviticus 25:23.

3. **God blesses those that bless Israel:** "And I will bless them that bless thee, and curse him that curseth thee: and in thee shall all families of the earth be blessed." Genesis 12:3.

4. **God gave the land of Israel to the Jews in an everlasting covenant:** "I will give your descendants all the land as an everlasting possession." Genesis 17:8.

5. **God promised to return the Jewish people back to their ancient land**: "For lo, the days come, saith the Lord, that I will bring again the captivity of my people Israel and Judah, saith the Lord; and I will cause them to return to the land that I gave to their fathers, and they shall possess it." Jeremiah 30:3.

6. **God promises to preserve Israel as a nation:** "Thus saith the Lord, which giveth the sun for a light by day, and the ordinances of the moon and of the stars for a light by night, which divideth the sea when the waves thereof roar; The Lord of Hosts is his name: If those ordinances depart from before me, saith the Lord, then the seed of Israel also shall cease from being a nation before me for ever." Jeremiah 31: 35–36.

7. **God judges any nation that comes against Israel:** "For the nation and kingdom that will not serve thee shall perish; yea, those nations shall be utterly wasted." Isaiah 60:12.

8. **God wants Jewish people to restore ancient ruins in the West Bank**: "Those from among you Shall build the old waste places; You shall raise up the foundations of many generations; and you

shall be called the Repairer of the Breach, the Restorer of Streets to Dwell In." Isaiah 58:12.

9. **God warns against changing ancient boundaries:** "Do not remove the ancient landmark which your fathers have set." Proverbs 22:28.

10. **God answered Abraham regarding Ishmael's inheritance, gave him 12 nations:** "And Abraham said to God, "Oh, that Ishmael might live before You!" Then God said: "...and as for Ishmael, I have heard you. Behold, I have blessed him, and will make him fruitful, and will multiply him exceedingly. He shall beget twelve princes, (nations) and I will make him a great nation." Genesis 17:18–21.

TOP TEN FUNDAMENTAL BIBLICAL TRUTHS
REPLACEMENT THEOLOGY DENIES

Infallibility: God's word is irrevocable. "So shall My word be that goes forth from My mouth; It shall not return to Me void, But it shall accomplish what I please, And it shall prosper *in the thing* for which I sent it." Isaiah 55:11.

Predestination: God preordains everything. "I say then, has God cast away His people? Certainly not! For I also am an Israelite, of the seed of Abraham, of the tribe of Benjamin. God has not cast away His people whom He foreknew." Romans 11: 1-2a.

Homogeneity: Jesus is of the Tribe of Judah. "But one of the elders said to me, "Do not weep. Behold, the Lion of the tribe of Judah, the Root of David, has prevailed to open the scroll and to loose its seven seals." Revelation 5:5.

Universality: God's covenant is universal. "Just as Abraham *"believed God, and it was accounted to him for righteousness* Therefore know that *only* those who are of faith are sons of Abraham. And the Scripture, foreseeing that God would justify the Gentiles by faith, preached the gospel to Abraham beforehand, *saying, "In you all the nations shall be blessed,* So then those who *are* of faith are blessed with believing Abraham." Galatians 3: 6–9.

Historicity: Christianity's roots are Hebraic roots. "And if some of the branches were broken off, and you, being a wild olive tree, were grafted in among them, and with them became a partaker of the root and fatness of the olive tree, do not boast against the branches. But if you do boast, *remember that* you do not support the root, but the root *supports* you. You will say then, "Branches were broken off that I might be grafted in." Romans 11: 17–19.

"For I do not desire, brethren, that you should be ignorant of this mystery, lest you should be wise in your own opinion, that blindness in part has happened to Israel until the fullness of the Gentiles has come in." Romans 11: 25.

Immutability: God's Covenant is Unchangeable. "And so all Israel will be saved as it is written: The Deliverer will come out of Zion, And

He will turn away ungodliness from Jacob; For this is My covenant with them, When I take away their sins Concerning the gospel *they are* enemies for your sake, but concerning the election *they are* beloved for the sake of the fathers. For the gifts and the calling of God *are* irrevocable." Romans 11: 26–29.

Jewishness of the Apostles. "The Jewish Apostles were messengers of the Gospel to the Gentiles. Then the eleven disciples went away into Galilee, to the mountain which Jesus had appointed for them. When they saw Him, they worshiped Him; but some doubted. And Jesus came and spoke to them, saying, "All authority has been given to Me in heaven and on earth. Go therefore and make disciples of all the nations, baptizing them in the name of the Father and of the Son and of the Holy Spirit, teaching them to observe all things that I have commanded you; and lo, I am with you always, even to the end of the age. Amen. "Matthew 28: 16–20.

Sovereignty. The supremacy of Gods will. "Know that whatever God does, It shall be forever. Nothing can be added to it, And nothing taken from it. God does it, that men should fear before Him." Ecclesiastes 3:14.

Perpetuity. The eternalness of His Covenant. "Thus God, determining to show more abundantly to the heirs of promise the immutability of His counsel, confirmed it by an oath, that by two immutable things, in which it is impossible for God to lie, we might have strong consolation, who have fled for refuge to lay hold of the hope set before us." Hebrews 6: 17–18.

Unconditionality. The covenant is a one-sided Divine initiative. "This is the covenant that I will make with them after those days, says the LORD: I will put My laws into their hearts, and in their minds I will write them then He adds, "Their sins and their lawless deeds I will remember no more." Hebrews 10: 16–17.

THE END OF THE GENTILE AGE

"And they will fall by the edge of the sword, and be led away captive into all nations. And Jerusalem will be trampled by Gentiles until the times of the Gentiles are fulfilled." Luke 21:24.

The period the Scriptures refers to as "the times of the Gentiles" can best be defined as a long period of Gentile control of Jerusalem and the Jewish people. This does not rule out temporary Jewish control such as exercised during the time of the Maccabbees, 164–63 BC; the First Revolt in 66–70 AD; the Second Revolt in 132–135 AD and 1948 to the present.

This period correlates concisely with the duration of the imperial domination of Israel by the seven-headed dragon of Revelation. Revelations shows a historical landscape of the times of the Gentiles from the beginning to the end. The heads of the dragon are Kingdoms that have ruled Israel through the centuries.

"But the angel said to me, "Why did you marvel? I will tell you the mystery of the woman and of the beast that carries her, which has the seven heads and the ten horns. ⁸ The beast that you saw was, and is not, and will ascend out of the bottomless pit and go to perdition. And those who dwell on the earth will marvel, whose names are not written in the Book of Life from the foundation of the world, when they see the beast that was, and is not, and yet is "Here is the mind which has wisdom: The seven heads are seven mountains on which the woman sits. There are also seven kings. Five have fallen, one is, and the other has not yet come. And when he comes, he must continue a short time. The beast that was, and is not, is himself also the eighth, and is of the seven, and is going to perdition.

The ten horns which you saw are ten kings who have received no kingdom as yet, but they receive authority for one hour as kings with the beast. These are of one mind, and they will give their power and authority to the beast. These will make war with the Lamb, and the Lamb will overcome them, for He is Lord of lords and King of kings; and those who are with Him are called, chosen, and faithfull. " **Revelation 17: 7–14.**

The seven heads of the beast are Egypt, Assyria, Babylon, Medo-Persia, Greece, Rome and finally the New World Order. When John was writing, he refers to the five as fallen. "The one that is" in the text was Rome, which was ruling in 96 AD. The seventh head is the New World Order, the last imperial domination of Jerusalem and the Modern State of Israel.

Biblical prophecy gives us a literal sequential view of history in advance, with amazing precision, not merely in a general sense but with complete details. The Bible is our time travel guide. You will see anew what must soon come to pass in these last days of the age of the Gentiles. These chronicles made in the distant past twenty eight centuries ago have never been proven wrong.

The period known as the times of the Gentiles will culminate with the battle of Armageddon. The armies of the Gentiles will finally be defeated by Christ while they are surrounding Jerusalem to exterminate the Jews for not abiding under the United Nations resolutions.

The battle lines have already been drawn. The current headlines signify the beginning of the terminal conflict. In order to understand what time it is and how close we are to the end of these times, background material is indispensable.

Let's take a quick look at the rebirth of Israel May 14, 1948 as a result of United Nations Resolutions 181 and 242.

The modern state of Israel exists today as a creation of the General Assembly of the United Nations, a body of Gentile nations. On December 11, 1948 the General Assembly drew the line in the sand when they made resolution 194: Article 7 defines the status of Jerusalem and Holy sites:

"It resolves that the Holy Places – including Nazareth – religious buildings and sites in Palestine should be protected and free access to them assured, in accordance with existing rights and historical practice; that arrangements to this end should be under effective United Nations supervision; that the United Nations Conciliation Commission, in presenting to the fourth regular session of the General Assembly its detailed proposals for a

permanent international regime for the territory of Jerusalem, should include recommendations concerning the Holy Places in that territory, that with regard to the Holy Places in the rest of Palestine the Commission should call upon the political authorities of the areas concerned to give appropriate formal guarantees as to the protection of the Holy Places and access to them, and that these undertakings should be presented to the General Assembly for approval.

It resolves that, in view of its association with three world religions, the Jerusalem area, including the present municipality of Jerusalem plus the surrounding villages and towns, the most eastern of which shall be Abu Dis: the most southern, Bethlehem, the most western, Ein Karim (including also the built-up area of Motsa); and the most northern Shu'fat, should be accorded special and separate treatment from the rest of Palestine and should be placed under effective United Nations control.

The ancient predictions accurately reveal the issue of Jerusalem end the Gentile age as these powers seek to enforce the United Nation resolutions in vain.

The burden of the word of the LORD against Israel. Thus says the LORD, who stretches out the heavens, lays the foundation of the earth, and forms the spirit of man within him: "Behold, I will make Jerusalem a cup of drunkenness to all the surrounding peoples, when they lay siege against Judah and Jerusalem. And it shall happen in that day that I will make Jerusalem a very heavy stone for all peoples; all who would heave it away will surely be cut in pieces, though all nations of the earth are gathered against it." **Zechariah 12: 1–3.**

The status of Jerusalem will close the Gentile age. Looking at the United Nations Resolution 303, we can see clearly it is in conflict with God's word. He will put His name in Jerusalem forever as a Jewish Holy City, yet the Gentile world openly challenges God's word. The United Nations believes the principles underlying its previous resolutions concerning this matter, and in particular its resolution of 29 November 1947, represent a just and equitable settlement of the question:

1. *To restate, therefore, its intention that Jerusalem should be placed under a permanent international regime, which should envisage appropriate guarantees for the protection of the Holy Places, both within and outside Jerusalem, and to confirm specifically the following provisions of General Assembly Resolution 181 (II) 3/ (1) the City of Jerusalem shall be established as a corpus separatum under a special international regime and shall be administered by the United Nations: (2) the Trusteeship Council shall be designated to discharge the responsibilities of the Administering Authority...; and (3) the City of Jerusalem shall include the present municipality of Jerusalem plus the surrounding villages and towns, the most eastern of which shall be Abu Dis; the most southern, Bethlehem; the most western, Ein Karim (including also the built-up areas of Motsa); and the most northern, Shu'fat...*

2. *To request for this purpose that the Trusteeship Council at its next session, whether special or regular, complete the preparation of the Statute of Jerusalem, omitting the now inapplicable provisions, Such as articles 32 and 39 and, without prejudice to the fundamental principles of the international regime for Jerusalem set forth in General Assembly resolution 181 (II) introducing therein amendments in the direction of its greater democratization, approve the Statue, and proceed immediately with its implementation. The Trusteeship Council shall not allow any actions taken by any interested Government or Governments to divert it from adopting and implementing the Statute of Jerusalem; II. Calls upon the States concerned to make formal undertaking, at an early date and in the light of their obligations as Members of the United Nations, that they will approach these matters with good will and be guided by the terms of the present resolution.*

God will destroy all nations (Gentile) that come against Jerusalem. On July 30, 1980 the Israeli Knesset passed the Jerusalem Law:

- *Jerusalem, complete and united, is the capital of Israel*

- *Jerusalem is the seat of the President of the State, the Knesset, the Government and the Supreme Court.*

- *The Holy Places shall be protected from desecration and any other violation and from anything likely to violate the freedom of access of the members of the different religions to the places sacred to them or their feelings towards those places.*

- *The Government shall provide for the development and prosperity of Jerusalem and the well-being of its inhabitants by allocation of special Funds, including a special annual grant to the Municipality of Jerusalem (Capital City Grant) with the approval of the Finance Committee of the Knesset*

- *Jerusalem shall be given special priority in the activities of the authorities of the State so as to further its development in economic and other matter*

- *The Government shall set up a special body or special bodies for the implementation of this section.*

The Jerusalem Basic Law sets the stage for the confrontation over Jerusalem.

In the 1967 Six-Day War, Israel took control of all Jerusalem including Temple Mount. After the Jerusalem Basic Law was passed by the Knesset Israel has made it clear Jerusalem is the eternal capital of the Jewish people and non-negotiable. They draw the line when it comes to their city.

Biblical prophetic chronology indicates that the New World Order will attack Jerusalem and enforce Resolution 303.

"And it shall come to pass in all the land," Says the LORD, " That two-thirds in it shall be cut off and die, But one-third shall be left in it: I will bring the one-third through the fire, Will refine them as silver is refined, And test them as gold is tested. They will call on My name, And I will answer them. I will say, 'This is My people'; And each one will say, 'The LORD is my God." **Zechariah 13: 8–9.**

"For I will gather all the nations to battle against Jerusalem; The city shall be taken, The houses rifled, And the women ravished. Half of the city shall go into captivity, But the

remnant of the people shall not be cut off from the city. Then the LORD will go forth And fight against those nations, As He fights in the day of battle." **Zechariah 14: 2–3.**

The United Nations will nullify the Jerusalem Basic Law and abolish Temple worship and set up a permanent regime over Jerusalem that will last for 42 months.

The Anti-Christ, the head of the New World Order will sit in the Third Temple acting as God and blaspheming God. During the construction of the Third Temple in the near future, the Dome of the Rock will remain. It stands at the court of the Gentiles. John saw in his vision the exclusion of the court of the Gentiles when the Third Temple is built.

> *"And he was given a mouth speaking great things and blasphemies, and he was given authority to continue for forty-two months."* Revelation 13:5.

> *"But leave out the court, which is outside the temple, and do not measure it, for it has been given to the Gentiles. And they will tread the holy city underfoot for forty-two months."* Revelation 11:2.

The Church will say there is not a need for another Temple. The church will claim that Israel has been rejected, cursed and condemned to death as Christ killers. They have no future in Gods economy. They lost that opportunity. Jerusalem no longer belongs to them. The whore Church will see the destruction of Jerusalem as a sign of divine approval of replacement theology. They will say God is judging them for building the Third Temple.

The current chain of events signals that the final countdown has begun. The battle lines have been drawn. The world stage is set for the last act to close. God will nullify Resolution 303 of the General Assembly of the United Nations. He will set up His Kingdom in Jerusalem for one thousand years.

This is a defining moment in history. The world is taking the wrong direction blinded by replacement theology and driven by age old Anti-Semitism. The present peace talks mark a final turning point and bring humankind to the brink of eternity. The world is already feeling the future shockwave of divine judgment with the global economic meltdown, unprecedented natural disasters, threats of nuclear devastation, the global energy crisis, the capital markets collapse, stock market upheaval, bank failures, credit implosion and global panic.

These cataclysmic events will continue to shake the foundations of Western civilization. The scope of these signs of the times will be so vast, so rapid, so varied that nation states will collapse paving the way for the New World Order. No nation will have enough resources to cope with both man-made and natural catastrophes.

The time has come to separate yourself from the whore church and heed the call of God.

> *"And I heard another voice from heaven saying, "Come out of her, my people, lest you share in her sins, and lest you receive of her plagues."* Revelation 18:4.

The church that denies the infallibility of the Holy Covenant makes God a liar and is a synagogue of Satan according to the Scriptures:

> *"I know your works, tribulation, and poverty (but you are rich); and I know the blasphemy of those who say they are Jews and are not, but are a synagogue of Satan."* Revelation 2:9.

Our God is still the God of Abraham, The Holy One of Israel and Jesus still the son of David, the Coming Messiah of Israel. He still blesses those who bless Israel.

> *"Now the LORD had said to Abram: "Get out of your country, From your family And from your father's house, To a land that I will show you. I will make you a great nation; I will bless you And make your name great; And you shall be a blessing. I will bless those who bless you, And I will curse him who curses you; And in you all the families of the earth shall be blessed."* Genesis 12: 1-3.

Bless Israel and be blessed by the Holy One of Israel. There is no inflation in Gods economy. The best of times lie ahead of those who take God at His word and reject false doctrines of demons and traditions of men.

> *"Have you not known? Have you not heard? The everlasting God, the LORD, The Creator of the ends of the earth, Neither faints nor is weary. His understanding is unsearchable. He gives power to the weak, And to those who have no might He increases strength. Even the youths*

shall faint and be weary, And the young men shall utterly fall, But those who wait on the LORD Shall renew their strength; They shall mount up with wings like eagles, They shall run and not be weary, They shall walk and not faint."
Isaiah 40: 28-31.

There is no lack in God during the worst of times in our global economy as God judges nations for violating the Holy Covenant. The people of God will be vindicated and blessed beyond measure. God promised to bless those who bless Israel. He is a promise keeper. He is faithful to His world. He said it. He will stand by His word forever. He will never change His mind.

"God is not a man, that He should lie, Nor a son of man, that He should repent.

Has He said, and will He not do? Or has He spoken, and will He not make it good?" Numbers 12:19.

There is nothing to worry about when you stand upon Gods word. There is nothing to fear, except fear itself, as long as you walk in obedience to His word. The blessings of God will continue to overwhelm you until the end. This promise is for you in this hour of crisis:

"Now it shall come to pass, if you diligently obey the voice of the LORD your God, to observe carefully all His commandments which I command you today, that the LORD your God will set you high above all nations of the earth. And all these blessings shall come upon you and overtake you, because you obey the voice of the LORD your God:

"Blessed shall you be in the city, and blessed shall you be in the country.

"Blessed shall be the fruit of your body, the produce of your ground and the increase of your herds, the increase of your cattle and the offspring of your flocks. "Blessed shall be your basket and your kneading bowl. "Blessed shall you be when you come in, and blessed shall you be when you go out. The LORD will cause your enemies who rise against you to be defeated before your face; they shall come out against you one way and flee before you seven ways."
Deuteronomy 28: 1-7.

Do not fear the end time, fear God and obey His world. He is in control of the endgame. The end of the times of the Gentiles is not your end you are now the spiritual seed of Abraham and a "joint heir and a citizen of the commonwealth of Israel."

> *"That at that time you were without Christ, being aliens from the commonwealth of Israel and strangers from the covenants of promise, having no hope and without God in the world. But now in Christ Jesus you who once were far off have been brought near by the blood of Christ. For He Himself is our peace, who has made both one, and has broken down the middle wall of separation, having abolished in His flesh the enmity, that is, the law of commandments contained in ordinances, so as to create in Himself one new man from the two, thus making peace, and that He might reconcile them both to God in one body through the cross, thereby putting to death the enmity."* **Ephesians 2: 12–16.**

> *"Now, therefore, you are no longer strangers and foreigners, but fellow citizens with the saints and members of the household of God."* Ephesians 2:19

The future belongs to you, the coming kingdom is yours. You are born again as a child of God. If you are not born again, you can become one by praying the prayer at the end of this chapter and receive Jesus Christ as Lord and Savor and escape the judgment of God. Do it now! Time is of essence.

As a child of God your end time manifest destiny is to pray for the children of Israel and for the Peace of Jerusalem as commanded in the Holy Scriptures.

> *"Pray for the peace of Jerusalem: May they prosper who love you."* Psalm 122:6.

> *"For Zion's sake I will not hold My peace, And for Jerusalem's sake I will not rest, Until her righteousness goes forth as brightness, And her salvation as a lamp that burns."* Isaiah 62:1.

> *"Son of man, I have made you a watchman for the house of Israel."* Ezekiel 3:17.

God's manifest destiny for Jerusalem and Israel is to make Jerusalem praise on the earth at the end of the times of the Gentiles when He sets up His kingdom in Jerusalem. And the saints that overcome will rule with him.

> *"And he who overcomes, and keeps My works until the end, to him I will give power over the nations— ' He shall rule them with a rod of iron;*
>
> *They shall be dashed to pieces like the potter's vessel as I also have received from My Father; and I will give him the morning star. "He who has an ear, let him hear what the Spirit says to the churches."* **Revelation 2: 26–29.**

MARANATHA! Come Lord Jesus.

SALVATION PRAYER

> *"But as many as received Him, to them He gave the right to become children of God, to those who believe in His name."* John 1:12

God will honor His word when you pray and believe in Jesus as your Savior. He will give you the power to become his child when you pray this prayer.

"Father God, I come to you in the name of your holy Son Jesus of Nazareth. I ask you to forgive me of all my sins. I accept Jesus Christ as my personal Savior and Lord. I ask you to cleanse me with His precious blood from all my sins. I believe that Jesus Christ is the Son of God who died for my sin. I will confess him before men as my Lord and Savior. I ask you to write my name in the book of life. According to your word grant me the power to become your son.

Thank you Father in Jesus Name my Lord and My Savior," Amen.